Amish Brides of Willow Creek

Book Two: Second Chances

Samantha Jillian Bayarr

www.LivingstonHallPublishers.blogspot.com

❧Second Chances❧

CHAPTER 1

"It's gone!"

Bethany tore the quilt off the bed and tossed the pillows onto the floor. She flung items out of the drawers of the antique bureau and threw it all on the floor at her feet.

"What are you looking for?" Levinia asked.

"Miriam stole *mei* car money."

"Let's not jump to conclusions," Levinia said trying to calm her frantic sister.

"I'm not jumping to conclusions. I *know* she took it!"

Bethany continued to throw things around the room they'd shared at the B&B, when she came across the empty paper bag the money was in. She wadded it up in a ball and pounded it with her fist. "Miriam warned us we'd be sorry just before she took *your* wedding dress and tried to marry your new husband in it! Now she's stolen *my* money. I had over five thousand dollars in this bag."

"Perhaps you should have given more thought to your actions before tossing chicken guts on her wedding dress," Levinia reprimanded.

"I only did it to defend *you!*"

"Ach, where did that get you? Now she's taken my wedding dress *and* your money."

Bethany tossed the wadded bag onto the bed.

"We need to go after her before she gets on the Greyhound Bus. Adam offered to drive her to the bus station to keep her from ruining your wedding. I'm sure he's gotten her there by now, but we can still catch her if she hasn't gotten on the bus back to Ohio."

"I have a feeling she's not going back to Ohio," Levinia said calmly. "Especially if she did take your money. For all we know, she may not even be getting on a bus. Hopefully Miriam is long-gone by now whether she has your money or not."

Bethany sank to the edge of the bed. "*Ach,* do you know how long I've been saving that money? I worked so hard for that money, and now it's gone."

Levinia didn't know how to comfort her distraught sister. She didn't even know how to get that kind of money back. It was more money than she'd probably seen in her lifetime.

"Let's get you home. Nate and I don't want to be out all night running you home."

Bethany sighed. "With you married now, Bess offered me the job here. Now that I am out of money, I think I'll take it. Besides, I'm still not ready to go home. *Daed* may have had a change of heart, but I need to know it's sincere before I commit to going back home."

Levinia nodded knowingly. "I suppose I don't blame you. If this doesn't work out, you can always fall back on your other idea."

Bethany looked at her curiously. "What idea?"

"Because *Daed* has had a change of heart, perhaps now would be a *gut* time to approach him about *mamm's* bakery. Especially if you don't intend to go back home right away. Talk to him about it now, so that if he gets angry, you won't have to live with him."

They both giggled.

"It's definitely something to think about," Bethany said. "Maybe I should bring it up after you give him the news of his first *grandkinner.*"

Levinia blushed. "*Ach,* we have only been married less than an hour, and already you have me pregnant? I honestly think I'd like to wait a year to have *mei* first *boppli* because I'd like to spend some time with *mei* new husband first."

Bethany giggled. "Well, I hear it takes about that long to have a *boppli,* so your plan will work out just fine for you!"

Levinia swatted in the air toward her sister.

"That isn't funny. I meant I wanted to wait at least a year before even getting pregnant."

"*Ach, gut* luck with that!"

Levinia shook her head. She wasn't going to admit that her sister knew more than she did when it came to men, but she was certainly eager to find out for herself. Levinia hated to see her younger sister so discouraged, but she had a new husband waiting for her.

"Speaking of which, *mei* new husband is waiting very patiently for us. Are you going or are you staying?"

Bethany let out a breath of defeat. "I suppose I have no choice but to stay. But are you sure you don't want to help me try to find Miriam and *mei* money?"

"I think we should leave all this in *Gott's* hands. If she took that money, *Gott* will find a way to get it back to you."

"I pray that you are right, dear *schweschder,*" Bethany said, blowing out another defeating breath.

CHAPTER 2

Miriam lurched forward, straining desperately to heave panicky gasps of air back into her lungs. Her face stung and her thoughts pulsated in correlation with the pain that engulfed her. Warmth dripped down the side of her face.

Blood.

Her ribcage would not yield to the shallow puffs of air she dragged in. Why couldn't she breathe? She felt wet earth beneath her fingertips, though she didn't comprehend her immediate surroundings. She listened, but all she could hear was the sound of her own cries.

Something floated down whimsically beside her.

Twenty-dollar-bills.

Several of them.

It was the money she'd stolen from Bethany to teach her a lesson. But why were they sailing through the air? Each bill assaulted her, whipping at her like sheets of rain in heavy wind.

What had she done?

Is Gott punishing me?

She clenched the bills, each one she could get her hands on. She scrambled across the ground gathering them with desperation.

Someone touched her shoulder.

Adam.

Her gaze focused on the commotion behind him.

An up-turned buggy, wheel still rolling.

She followed the trail of tire marks on the wet pavement to a small car that had careened off into the ditch.

They'd been hit by a car.

Miriam staggered toward the downed horse.

He lifted his head and struggled to get to his feet.

He was alright, just trapped beneath the harnesses that bound him to the overturned buggy.

Was *she* alright?

Her shoulder hurt. Her face stung. Her head pounded.

She let the money drop to her feet and lifted a hand to her face. She touched her cheek, running her fingers down a laceration the full length of her face. She pulled her hand away, bringing her wet fingers up in front of her to examine them.

Blood.

Lots of it.

"Miriam, you're hurt. Sit down."

It was Adam's voice she heard, but she wasn't comprehending what he was trying to say to her.

Was she hurt? She didn't know.

She guessed it would account for the blood and the pain she felt. Or did she? Her vision was dizzying, and it confused her.

Sirens interrupted her thoughts, if she really had any that made any sense. Looking down at the money swirling about her feet, she bent to pick it up.

She'd lost a shoe.

"I can't find my shoe," she said frantically.

"I'll find it for you," Adam offered. "But first, let the paramedics take a look at you."

People were talking to her, but she didn't want their help. She needed to find her shoe.

And she needed to find the rest of the money so she could return it to Bethany.

She still had Levinia's wedding dress.

She would never have a use for it.

She would never love again.

Miriam succumbed to the dizziness, then all went black.

CHAPTER 3

Miriam tried to move, but everything ached. She fluttered her heavy lashes.

Someone was talking to her.

"We were unable to give you anything but non-narcotic pain meds because of the pregnancy," a female voice said while holding Miriam's wrist.

Miriam forced her eyes open, focusing on a nurse taking her pulse.

"W-what?" Miriam whispered.

The nurse let her wrist drop gently against the bed and made a note in her chart.

"I said, you might still be in a lot of pain because we can't give you anything stronger than Tylenol for the pain because of your pregnancy. We did an ultrasound and everything is just fine. That little one is tough to survive that accident." The nurse stopped to look at Miriam, who had said nothing. "You're about twelve weeks along. You did know you were pregnant, didn't you?"

Miriam closed her eyes.

She couldn't answer.

She was too ashamed to face the truth she had ignored until now.

She knew she was pregnant.

The test had come up positive.

It was the reason she'd tried to force Nate to marry her. She knew that if she were to marry the father of her child, an *Englischer,* she would lose the family she'd been adopted into. It was the only family she'd ever known, and she feared her actions had caused her to lose them. Without an Amish husband, she would have to leave the community.

It didn't matter now.

She'd already been banned.

She now knew she would not have been able to convince anyone that the child was Nate's. She was too far along. When she'd thought up the crazy plan, she'd had no idea how far along she was. Now, she had no idea what she was going to do with herself or even what she would do with a child. She was just a child, herself—barely twenty, and unwed. Tears ran down her cheeks from her closed eyes, as she listened to the nurse leave the room.

She was all alone.

And that was how she would be—even with a baby to care for. A million thoughts ran through her head. Her own mother had given her away. Had her mother been in the same bad spot she was in? Had her birth-mother made the same mistake she had made? She would have to do the same thing to her child that was done to her—she would have to give the child up to strangers to raise.

She had no other choice.

She couldn't take care of a child without a husband. She had no job and no money. The Amish family that adopted her would not help her care for the child. They would try to force her to marry the father of the child, but when they discovered he was an *Englischer,* that would be the end of her relationship with her family. It didn't matter because Ray would never marry her now that she had hurt him so badly.

She no husband, no job, no roof over her head, no money, and no hope.

Even the money she'd stolen from Bethany was gone—blown away in the streets after the accident. Her intention was just to borrow the money, and she was going to send it back to her after she'd gotten settled into a place and gotten a job. Now it was gone, and not only would she have to find a way to pay back that money, but she would also have to find a way to support herself now that she'd left home.

She could never go back now—she would be shunned if she wasn't already.

Where was she to go?

She needed a place to stay, but there would be no one in this community that would take her in after the Bishop ran her out of the community. Not to mention the fact she was pregnant out of wedlock.

What was she to do?

She couldn't go home to Ohio, and she couldn't stay here in Indiana. She certainly couldn't stay in this hospital too much longer. Sooner or later, even *they* would make her leave.

Tears filled her eyes. She'd made a mess of her life, and now she'd made a mess of the life of an innocent child just as her own mother had. She always told herself she would not grow up to be like the woman who had given her away, but here she was in the same predicament. Her child would suffer from her mistakes, just as she had suffered from her birth-mother's mistakes. It just wasn't fair. Was *Gott* punishing her? Had *Gott* had a reason to punish her own birth mother for the same reason?

Miriam placed her hands over her abdomen and sobbed even harder. "I'm so sorry I did this to you. I was trying to grow up too soon, and now I've made a mess of both our lives. I hope you understand that I can't take care of you. Please forgive me for wrecking your life before it really starts. I hope someday you can forgive me."

She was sobbing so hard she could barely get the words out, but they were too important not to say.

She wondered if her own mother had spoken the same words to *her* before she'd given her up. She would have liked to have known her mother, and especially the reason the woman had let her go. She'd always resented her birth mother for giving her up, and thought of her as a coward who took the easy way out. But she was beginning to understand that perhaps what her birth mother had done was the bravest, most responsible thing she could have done for Miriam.

If Miriam had her way, she would be married, and keeping her child would not be a second thought—it would be an automatic one. One that she wouldn't even have to consider because it would be a given that she would raise her child.

But now—well, now things were different.

She couldn't keep her child—that was the given.

CHAPTER 4

"Miriam, you have a visitor," her nurse said. "Do you feel up to seeing anyone?"

She didn't respond.

She didn't care.

With her back to the door, she continued to stare out the window at the cold, October wind blowing sheets of rain sideways. It was a miserable day to match her miserable mood.

Hearing footsteps, she pulled the bed-sheet over her face, hoping to hide the large bandage that covered her cheek from the corner of her right eye to just below her chin. She'd been told that her face had suffered a tear that had required thirty-seven stitches, and would most likely leave her scarred for life.

On top of everything else, she'd been stripped of the one thing she had always been sure of—her physical beauty. It was what she felt linked her to her birth-mother, from whom she was a mirror likeness. Her adoptive mother had given her a photograph when Miriam was young—before the woman had passed away giving birth to her own child.

Miriam had an older brother, her adoptive parent's natural child. Her adoptive mother had suffered many miscarriages since his birth, and was not supposed to have any more children, but she'd become pregnant again. Thinking she was out of the woods at full-term, she'd suffered unforeseen complications. She and the baby had both perished, leaving Miriam at the age of seven to be raised by her adoptive father and brother who was four years her senior.

Miriam wasn't up for any more pain or heartache. And she certainly wasn't in the mood for anyone to come and gloat over her misfortune. The only people she knew in this town disliked her, and they would certainly ridicule her over her present appearance.

She heard the padding of soft footsteps entering her room.

"Go away," she whispered.

"I was hoping to meet you sooner, and under different circumstances," a kind, female voice said quietly. "But I only just learned you were here in Indiana."

Miriam didn't respond. She assumed the woman would realize she'd walked into the wrong room and leave just as quickly as she'd come in.

"I'm Claudia, Ray's mom. With Ray back in Ohio with his dad, I thought this would give us an opportunity to get to know one another."

Miriam felt her heart make a sudden somersault behind her ribcage. What was Ray's mother doing here, and what did she want with

Miriam? Didn't she know she and Ray had broken up?

"How did you know I was here?" Miriam asked the woman without turning around.

"Your friend, Nate called looking for Ray and explained you were here. He thought Ray might want to see you."

My friend, Nate? That's funny! He's never been a friend. If Nate sent word to Ray, then he must know I'm pregnant. She's only here because she knows about the baby.

Humiliation rose up in Miriam. The last thing she wanted was for this woman to meddle in her business. It was tough enough on her to sort this out for the best interest of her and the baby. But now, she would have someone trying to influence her decision when her mind was already made up.

"You shouldn't have come. I'm sorry you wasted your time, but I'm giving up the baby and no one is going to make me change my mind. It's what is best for it. I don't know how to be a mother because I never really had one, and I certainly can't support a child—I have no money and no job and nowhere to even go when they kick me out of here."

The woman sat down in the chair beside the bed and placed a gentle hand on Miriam's arm. "I didn't know you were pregnant. I only came here because Ray had told me so much about you. He loves you very much."

"He doesn't love me anymore," Miriam said with a shaky voice. "I hurt him by trying to marry another man. Didn't he tell you what a mess I've made of everything?"

Miriam choked back tears that seemed to want to flow despite every effort she made to stop them. She felt the woman's hand patting her arm gently.

"He told me about that, but I figured you probably had a pretty good reason for doing what you did. Especially since Nate is such a good friend to you still that he would call to let Ray know how you were doing."

"He probably just wanted to humiliate me. He was probably hoping Ray would come and see me at my worst. I've got a huge gash in my face that is going to leave an ugly scar, and I'm knocked up and all alone. What better revenge could Nate find against me than the mess I've made of my own life?"

"When I got pregnant for Ray, I was alone and scared like I'm sure you are right now. I wasn't married to his father, and I was only seventeen years old. My parents tried to make me give him up, but I thought it was best to keep him and raise him myself. I can't say it wasn't tough raising him alone. It certainly would have been easier if his father had married me, but he wasn't in love with me. He wanted another girl. He married her, and they were divorced a year later. But at that time, Ray's father decided to take an active role in his life. Even though we couldn't make it work as a family, we did manage to raise him together. He's better off for it, I think. Ray says so.

He knows I was a young unwed mother and faced with having to give him up for adoption. He says he's glad I kept him, but he also knows it wasn't easy for me. Did I make the right decision? There is really no way of ever knowing that because I don't know if he and I would have been better off if I'd let someone else raise him. Times were tough, but the love was always there. It sounds as if you've made up your mind, but if you should change it, I'd be willing to help you.

My parents didn't support my decision, and they let me do it alone. I believe if I'd had someone to help me through raising a child on my own, it might not have been such a struggle. But I would do it all over again if I had to. Keeping a child and raising it on your own is not an easy decision, and certainly not for one who is weak. It takes a strong person to handle that kind of responsibility."

"I don't think I'm that strong," Miriam muttered under her breath.

"Ray is that strong," she said.

"He doesn't want me in his life. No one does. I'm shunned from the community here, and I will be shunned from my own community if I try to return home. I only wanted to marry Nate because he is Amish and I didn't want to be alone and lose my adopted family. If I married an *Englischer* I would have lost them. But none of that matters now because I've already lost them. I have no family now."

"Since you are carrying my son's child; that makes *us* family," Claudia said in a comforting tone.

Miriam turned slowly in the hospital bed, wincing against the pain that still pounded in her head. Focusing on the woman sitting beside her, she noticed right away that Ray had the same coarse blonde hair, and his eyes were the same greenish-blue. She seemed young, but Miriam supposed that was due to the young age at which she'd had Ray.

Could she trust this woman? She almost didn't have any other choice. Still, she didn't want the woman taking an interest in helping her simply because she didn't want Miriam giving up her son's child for adoption. She couldn't raise a child when she had no idea of where she was even going to live, or how she was going to survive without a job. There would be no help from the community because of the pregnancy; that was for sure and for certain.

CHAPTER 5

Miriam stood in the bathroom of her hospital room staring blankly at her reflection in the mirror. Her eye was blackened, bits of green filling in the curve just under her lashes. Her eye itself was bloodshot, and her vision was a little blurry. Would she lose her eyesight? The doctor hadn't said anything to her about it, but he also hadn't told her how bad she looked either.

Though she wanted to see just how bad the cut on her face was, she reasoned with herself that what she didn't know couldn't hurt her. Once she saw what was under the bandage, there would be no way to take back what she'd seen.

She was already a little freaked out over what she *could* see. It was the part hidden under the bandage that terrified her the most. Her cheek was physically painful, and she figured that was not a good sign.

She continued to stare at the unrecognizable reflection staring back at her. She was never going to be the same in any way—no matter what lay beneath the bandage. Even if she didn't have the cut on her face, she feared what having a baby was going to do to her figure. She'd seen what it had done to several of the girls her age. She wasn't ready for her entire life to change.

Gott, I don't know if I'm ready for this, but I pray that you will give me the strength to get through it. Take away the selfishness and anger I feel right now. Help me to make the right decision for the baby that I'm carrying. And please put forgiveness in the hearts of those I've hurt with my carelessness.

Miriam winced as she lifted trembling fingers to the edge of the bandage that covered most of the right side of her face. She slowly folded down the edge, hoping to see something, but all she saw was more discoloration and bruising. She wiggled her face a little feeling the tug of the stitches that limited movement of the skin. It felt tight and stiff—almost unnatural.

What had they done to her face?

Closing her eyes, she tugged lightly at the bandage, pulling down toward her chin until she'd removed the entire piece of gauze. She was terrified to open her eyes—terrified to the point it was making her nauseous.

But she *had* to see—*had* to know.

No matter how terrible it was, she had to see what had happened to her in that accident. Slowly lifting her gaze, she blurred her vision and looked only in her eyes. She allowed her gaze to drift down her face, not comprehending what she saw.

She pulled a trembling hand to her mouth, shock rendering her speechless.

It was far worse than she'd thought.

She stifled a strangled cry, swallowing hard the reality of her reflection.

I'm hideous!

Thick black stitches pulled the sides of her cheek together, holding her skin so taught it caused her pain.

"Why did they have to use stitches that were so noticeable?" she sobbed.

She could see little holes along the cut where the thick stitching laced her face back together. Were they permanent? What if makeup wouldn't cover the scar? Was she doomed to look like this for the rest of her life? She was too young to have her life so ruined. How was she ever going to feel normal again?

She padded her way back to her bed and slumped down against the hard mattress—not caring about the pain it caused her. She hadn't even bothered to cover her face back up. What was the use in it? She was forever ugly. Might as well get the world used to seeing her now so they could gasp and get it over with.

She was numb with sadness and self-pity.

She was alone and pregnant—and ugly.

A knock to her door startled her. She was not in the mood for another visit from Claudia at the moment.

"Go away," she said sniffling.

"I came to see how you were doing," a male voice said.

Miriam turned halfway around to see who it was.

It was Adam.

He was the *last* person she wanted to see right now.

This was all *his* fault.

Miriam whipped her aching head around and pointed to her stitched-up face. "You want to see how I'm doing? *This* is how I'm doing! I'm scarred for life thanks to you!"

Tears ran down her face, and she winced as they stung her wound. "If you had been paying more attention to the road than to me, then that car wouldn't have hit us."

"I'm sorry. I was only trying to talk to you. I only—"

"I didn't want you to talk to me! I wanted you to leave me alone," she screamed at him.

"I was only trying to help you. I felt bad that you were being run out of the community. I wanted to help you find a way to stay because—"

"Because what?" she interrupted. "Because you thought I was pretty?"

"Well—*jah,*" Adam admitted.

She turned her face more toward him. "I'm not so pretty now, am I?"

"That cut doesn't change how beautiful you are."

"Are you kidding me?" she sobbed. "It changes everything!"

"It doesn't change anything in *my* eyes. But that wasn't the *only* reason I was hoping you would stay. I believe that everyone deserves a second chance."

"A second chance for what? I lied to trick your cousin into marrying me."

"I think I know why you did it," he said cautiously.

She pursed her lips and narrowed her eyes. "And why is that?"

"Because you're pregnant. If you marry an Amish *mann* you can remain in the community. But if you marry the *Englischer,* Ray, who is probably the *daed,* then you would fall under the ban."

"It doesn't matter now," she sobbed. "I've already lost my family."

"You don't have to," Adam offered gingerly.

"When my brother comes to take me back home, he will find out then, and he will return to our community without me."

"What if you stay here instead?"

Miriam flashed him a confused look. "I can't. The Bishop has banned me from this community. It's only a matter of time before my own community is sent word of my actions."

"You can stay here if you are married."

"Nate married Levinia—or did you forget?"

"I will marry you," Adam said.

"Why would *you* marry me when your cousin refused?"

He hung his head. "I suppose I feel I owe you—because of the accident."

Miriam considered his words carefully. She was facing being homeless and pregnant and scarred for life with no possibility of ever marrying. She was desperate. Marrying Adam might just work. She didn't love him, but he didn't love her either. He was attractive, and a hard worker. There was real possibility there.

Could she go through with such a plan?

She'd been prepared to make the same mistake only two days ago, but she'd done that without even thinking. Now that she'd had time to think about it, she wasn't so certain it was the right thing to do. But the problem still remained of her pregnancy. If she married, she could keep her child *and* her family.

It saddened her to realize that this was what her life had become, but she felt she had no other choice.

Miriam looked up at Adam, tears pooling in her eyes. "Alright, I'll marry you!"

CHAPTER 6

"You must keep this bandage on your wound," the nurse reprimanded Miriam. "If it gets infected, it is more likely to scar."

"What does it matter?" Miriam mumbled. "It's going to be a terrible scar no matter what."

"Infection won't be good for the baby, and neither will the medicine we will have to give you. All that will be harsh on the baby's system. So let's keep this covered up so we can avoid all of that."

Her nurse was a little short with her, but Miriam knew she was only trying to protect her and the baby. It was hard to think about that right now though. With the decision of marrying Adam weighing on her, she had little room to think of anything else at the moment.

Another knock sounded at the door.

Do people not understand I want to be left alone?

"Good afternoon," came Claudia's cheery voice. "How are you feeling today?"

Miriam looked over at her and grunted her answer.

"That good, huh?"

Miriam couldn't even force a smile, knowing the movement of her face would cause her pain.

"I saw you had company a little bit ago and thought I'd go down to the cafeteria for a cup of coffee until the young man left. But I couldn't help but overhear your conversation. I wasn't trying to eavesdrop, but I kind of did out of concern for you and the baby."

"Well then you already know that I agreed to marry Adam so I could stay in the Amish community."

"I wish I could say I understood what being part of an Amish community means to you, but I don't," Claudia admitted. "But you don't have to make that decision right away."

Miriam shrugged. "I should make it soon because I will begin to show in my pregnancy soon. My brother will be here in a few days and he will know. He will enforce the marriage in my father's absence or he will shun me."

Miriam began to cry all over again.

Claudia patted her gently, offering her a tissue from her purse. "I wanted to offer you another alternative to marrying Adam."

Miriam's ears perked up. She would listen, but she was pretty well determined to marry Adam. Even though she was torn between being Amish and *Englisch,* she feared losing the only family she'd ever known. Just because her birth mother was *Englisch,* did not mean she knew what it was like to be *Englisch.* All she knew was being Amish.

"I'd like to offer you a place to stay while you recover," Claudia began. "I have a guest room that has never been used, and I think you could be very comfortable there for however long you want to stay. I also have a gift shop in town, and I could use some help there once you are back on your feet in a week or so. I can give you a place to stay and a job for as long as you want them."

"What about Adam?" Miriam asked. "He will want to court me until we are married. Won't it be uncomfortable for you to see us together? I will want to court him even while I'm deciding for sure and for certain."

Claudia shook her head. "It won't be a problem for Adam to come *calling* for you. I will do everything I can to make him feel welcome."

Miriam looked at Claudia wondering if there was a *catch* to her offer, but she hadn't mentioned any house-rules for her. Perhaps she should ask if she expected anything of her while she was a guest in her home.

"Do you have any rules I should know about so I don't accidentally break any while I'm there?"

Claudia smiled. "You are a grown woman who is about to be a mother. I don't think it's necessary to put any strict rules on you. As long as we respect each other's space, I think we will get along just fine."

"I'm used to rules," Miriam said. "The Ordnung is nothing but rules." She patted her belly. "Obviously I broke a few of them."

"I'm not here to judge you. I just want to help you and my grandchild to have the best possible outcome."

There it was—the *catch*. She had a vested interest in Miriam because of the child she carried. She prayed she wasn't making a big mistake by agreeing to stay with Claudia. But just like with Adam; right now, she had no other choice.

CHAPTER 7

"Why are you marrying that woman?" Libby asked. "She has done nothing but cause trouble for everyone here."

Adam followed his sister into the chicken coop. He knew what Libby said was right, but he felt obligated to take care of Miriam anyway. His carelessness could have caused the loss of her baby. As it were, the woman would have to live with a scar on her face for the rest of her life. Would she resent him for that? She would see it every day. Would she ever be able to forgive him? Perhaps not, but marrying her might make a difference.

"I owe her for what I did to her."

Libby shook her head with frustration. "It was an accident. You don't owe her anything. She owes Bethany a lot of money though. She is a thief and a liar, and she's hurt your cousin and his new *fraa*. What does Nate even have to say about your decision?"

Adam lowered his head. "I haven't had the nerve to tell him yet."

"*Ach,* that right there should tell you that you shouldn't marry her. Let her marry the *boppli's daed.*"

"I'm marrying her so she can stay in the community."

Libby adjusted the egg basket in her hand, reaching under another hen and feeling for an egg. "That is the wrong reason to marry someone. Don't you want to marry someone you love?"

"I could learn to love her," he said in his defense. "And she could learn to love me. We could have a *gut* marriage if we try."

"She's a selfish woman, *bruder,* don't kid yourself about that. She eagerly agreed to let you marry her for that very reason. She was only thinking of herself. She is what the *Englisch* call an opportunist."

"What do you mean by that?"

"It means she saw an opportunity in you, and she took it. But you handed it right over to her."

Adam felt under one of the hens and pulled out an egg, dropping it in Libby's basket. "She's not as bad as you think she is."

Libby narrowed her gaze on Adam. "Perhaps you should look beyond her pretty face and into her not-so-pretty soul."

Adam placed another egg into the basket. "That is not for you to judge. I think everyone deserves a second chance."

"I'm not convinced Miriam deserves anything from anyone, but you are right. That is not for me to judge. If it means that much to you, I will try to give her some consideration—but only because she is to be your *fraa* soon."

Libby had made her way to the end of the chicken coop and let herself out the door, Adam on her heels. "When is the wedding? Will it be quick and quiet, or will you be having an open wedding with the community?"

Adam hadn't thought that far ahead. His main concern was how his *daed* was going to divide his property so he would have a place to live with Miriam once they were wed. He didn't put much stock in the wedding itself as he did about supporting her and a *boppli* so soon. It wouldn't take but a few days to put up a basic house on the far end of his *daed's* acreage, but he also needed help from the very community that had shunned Miriam to get them started with their new life together. He worried the community would not be so willing to shower them with the usual gifts to set up their house, or food to start them off for the winter that was already on its way.

Adam shouldered out into the cold, November wind. Right on cue, as if the first day of November was required to turn to winter, the wind and icy rain assaulted him as he made his way to the barn for the morning milking.

Normally he spent the morning milking in prayer, but today, he had a lot of thinking to do. Perhaps marrying Miriam was going to be tougher than he originally thought. It was too late to take it back now. He'd made a promise to her, and he was a man of his word. He owed her, and if that meant defending her to a community that rejected her, he'd have to do whatever it took to change their minds about her.

His own parents hadn't been too happy about the idea of him marrying her. He had led them to believe he was the father of the child she carried, which wasn't easy considering Miriam had only just tried to marry his cousin less than a week ago. He didn't enjoy deceiving his family this way, but he felt an obligation to Miriam that they just wouldn't understand.

A cold draft whirling through the barn interrupted Adam's thoughts. Nate walked up to him and stared at him for a moment.

"I ran into Libby on the way in here. Is it true? You're to marry Miriam? After what she did to Levinia and Bethany and me?"

Adam crouched down on the milking stool in front of Buttercup and began to milk her. "Don't make me defend my decision to you. My mind is already made up."

Nate leaned up against the stall. "I won't put you on the defensive end of my opinions, but I will tell you to be certain you know what you're up against. She's a handful, and if you're not sure about this, she could make your life miserable. If you change your mind, I'm here. If you go through with it, I'm still here for you."

"I appreciate the show of support. I'm going to need it when the community finds out my plans."

"Have you thought about what you will do if you don't get the support of the Bishop and the community?"

Adam didn't have an answer for his cousin. He had no idea what he would do if pushed by the Bishop to choose between his obligation to Miriam and his commitment to the community. He hadn't thought that his offer of marriage could get him shunned when he'd made the offer to her. He supposed if it came down to it, Miriam would back out if it meant she would not be able to remain in the community. Wouldn't she?

CHAPTER 8

Miriam folded her things neatly and tucked them into the broken suitcase that Adam had salvaged from the wreckage after the accident. With trembling hands she tucked away her parting instructions from the hospital.

Her parting instructions.

They had just released her and she still hadn't decided if she would accept Claudia's offer to recover at her home. Deep down, she knew she had no other choice. But she wasn't ready to leave the hospital, even though they'd told her repeatedly how lucky she was, and that there was no medical reason to keep her. If mental anguish counted, they'd keep her here forever. But unfortunately, her state of mind seemed to be the only thing preventing her from accepting the final diagnosis.

She'd tried to insist that more tests be run on her to be certain she hadn't suffered anything internal they might have missed. After all, being thrown from a buggy could have caused all sorts of damage to her internal organs. No matter how many questions she asked, and how much she pressed the hospital staff, they didn't agree with her requests for a more in-depth analysis of her complaints.

Now, after a week of being here, she'd gotten used to the busy noises of the hospital that never seemed to quiet. The constant bustle that made her aware that someone was always up watching over her had become comforting. She'd felt safe here—protected. Now, the very thought of having to travel by car to Claudia's house filled her with an uneasiness she just couldn't shake.

Her stomach knotted, she dreaded leaving, but she continued to pack the things they'd given her to take *home* with her. Adam had offered to pick her up, but she was more willing to ride in Claudia's car than in a buggy for now. She wondered if she would ever be able to ride in a buggy again. The thought of it made her shudder.

Right on cue, Claudia appeared in the doorway of her hospital room as if magnetized to Miriam's thoughts. She crossed the room and tucked her into a soft embrace. But for Miriam, who hadn't welcomed the awkward contact, anxiety and a suffocating feeling ensued.

Miriam struggled to escape the unnatural embrace Claudia had drawn her into. This was not normal for her—a mother's solace. There had not been any affection for her—no patience—no love, since her adoptive mother had passed.

It was something she dearly missed.

At her *mamm's* funeral, she'd flung herself across the primitive, pine box where her *mamm* lay all-too-silent, begging her *mamm* not to leave her.

Daed had scooped her up by her middle and dragged her off, balancing her against his side while she'd kicked and screamed like a squealing piglet. The last thing she'd remembered of that day was being tossed in the back of *Daed's* buggy with no one to hold her. The stern look of disapproval over her behavior separated them. There was no comfort for her—only stifled tears. There would be no respite from the pain and solitude that would become her life. It was that day that she'd accepted he wasn't her real father.

Claudia let her go and moved to pick up her suitcase. "Did you hear from your brother?"

"*Jah*—yes. He is going to be here at the end of the week, but my father is not coming."

Claudia patted Miriam's arm cautiously. "Do they know of your plans to marry *Adam*?"

Miriam nodded. "Benjamin is not as stern as my father, and so he is eager to attend the wedding. I didn't tell him the rest of the story. I figured that was best said in person."

She could tell Claudia wasn't happy with her answer, but she had only agreed to give her decision some added thought.

"Just because I'm marrying Adam does not mean you will not be able to be a part of the baby's life. Adam agreed to allow Ray the liberty of seeing the child."

Claudia didn't look convinced.

"The Amish are a peaceful people. It is what keeps me bound to this life. When I met Ray, I thought I was missing out on something because I never knew my birth-mother, who was an *Englischer*. I thought I wanted to be like her, but now—" she patted her abdomen. "Now that I'm pregnant, I want to change that for my child. I want to raise my child with Amish values."

"I'm trying to understand," Claudia said. "But I think you can raise your child with those values whether you raise it in an English household or an Amish one. The Amish is in your heart, not in your blood."

Miriam hadn't thought of it that way before. She'd spent the remainder of her childhood after her *mamm* died struggling to know where she fit in. Though she admired and craved the Amish lifestyle and values, the *Englisch* blood coursing through her veins seemed to stir up rebellion in her. Because of that, she feared raising her child in an uncontrolled environment away from the rules of the Ordnung.

"I don't want my child to repeat the mistakes I have made. I repeated the same pattern as my birth-mother, but I will not give up my child like she did. I'm certain she did what she thought was best for me, but I want to see what making the other choice will do for *my* child."

"But you were raised in an Amish household, and you still became pregnant out of wedlock. How do you think you can change that for your child?"

Miriam shrugged.

She didn't have an answer that was logical. The thing she feared most was dying when the child was young and leaving it behind to fend for itself the way her own *mamm* had done.

CHAPTER 9

Miriam stood in the doorway of the room in which she'd been welcomed to stay. In her mind, the arrangement was only temporary—until the wedding next week. Miriam was eager to get the wedding over with soon—before she began showing her pregnancy.

Claudia didn't seem to have the same sense of urgency that Miriam had. She still talked of Miriam working in her gift shop downtown, and had even made open plans for a homecoming dinner for Ray tomorrow evening.

Miriam wasn't so certain she was ready to face Ray, but she knew it was inevitable. If she had her way, she'd avoid him indefinitely, but she'd promised his mother that she'd give him the news of the pregnancy, and offer him the option to be a part of the child's life.

It would not be easy for her to stifle her feelings, but she'd convinced herself she was doing what was best for her child. She was confused, and very torn between doing what was right, and what she thought was best for her child. Deciding to be unselfish for a change, she opted to consider the best course of action for the child she carried. And that, she felt, was to remain in the Amish community.

Placing her suitcase on the bed, Miriam picked up a tailor-made, Amish doll tucked in front of the pillows. She turned it over, reading the tag boasting its manufacturer.

Made in China.

Miriam understood that Claudia was only trying to make her feel *at home,* but to her, the doll was nothing short of an insult. It wasn't authentic. It wasn't Amish-made. She sat on the edge of the fancy, store-bought quilt that draped the bed in more insult, and stared at the doll in her hands.

Mamm had taught her how to make dolls when she was only four years old. She and *mamm* had sewn a doll for each of her twelve cousins the Christmas just before she'd died. Miriam pulled at the taught stitching, ripping it without thinking. She looked up, noticing Claudia standing in the doorway, watching her.

"Forgive me," she said holding up the doll. "I didn't mean to rip it. If you have a needle and thread, I'll sew it. Or I can make you an authentic one instead."

"Authentic?" Claudia repeated.

"Made by the Amish."

She showed Claudia the tag in the back.

"This one was made in China. Wouldn't you rather have one made by the Amish?"

Claudia reached for the doll. "I suppose I never thought about where it was made. I sell them in my store, and I've never had anyone complain about it."

Miriam chuckled. "You sell those in your store?"

"Uh-huh, why?"

"Because I could make them for you, and you could make more money selling authentic Amish-made dolls. The material to make these is very inexpensive."

Claudia smiled warmly. "How about if I get you some material, and you can sell them at the store yourself. You can have all the profits from it because they will probably drive in additional business for me if I have *authentic* Amish-made dolls in my store."

"*Danki.* I could use some money with the baby coming. I can't expect Adam to take on all the responsibility. Besides, I owe someone some money."

Claudia looked as if she wanted Miriam to elaborate on her comments, but she wasn't willing to say any more than she already had. She'd already said too much.

She stretched and forced a yawn, hoping the older woman would get the hint.

Thankfully she did.

"I'll leave you to get settled in. Let me know if you need anything. Otherwise, I'll check in on you after a little while."

She shot her an awkward smile and exited the room.

Miriam knew she'd hurt her feelings, but she needed some alone-time if she was going to rehearse what she would say to Ray when she saw him tomorrow at dinner. Her stomach roiled at the thought of it, but it was a necessary meeting.

How had her life suddenly become so complicated?

In the course of one summer, she'd managed to compromise her virtue, become pregnant, and ended the season by becoming scarred for life. In retrospect, all of it had scarred her for life—not just the physical cut down her face. Her life was never going to be the same.

She wondered if she could ever love Adam the way she loved Ray. She was so numb from all the physical and emotional pain of the last couple of months, it was a wonder she could even think at all.

Her thoughts wandered to the first time she'd met Ray. He was so handsome, and Miriam was immediately smitten with him. He'd been so kind and understanding, she couldn't help but fall for him. No one in the Amish community had understood her except her *mamm*.

But Ray understood her.

He understood the pain she'd suffered when she'd lost her *mamm*. He even understood her need to find her birth mother. He'd been such a good listener, he'd nearly made her forget her troubles. And when he held her—that was when she'd forgotten everything, including her morals.

Ray had a way of helping her to understand herself. She trusted him. In fact, she'd trusted him with her innermost secrets. Things she'd never told anyone. Not because it was too secret to tell, but because until she'd met Ray, she'd had no real friends. She'd always had plenty of cousins around, but she could never tell them anything she didn't want getting back to *Daed* in some way or another.

Ray had been an exception. He had been more than a boyfriend. He had been a true friend to her.

She blew out a heavy sigh.

How was she going to live without him?

She hadn't thought that far ahead.

Hadn't thought about it even when she'd risked everything to try to trick Nate into marrying her.

Now that she'd agreed to marry Adam, she would lose Ray all over again, and it hurt more than she ever thought it could.

CHAPTER 10

Miriam trembled when she heard Ray's truck pull into his mother's driveway. Panicking, she crossed the room to the mirror above the long dresser and stared at her reflection. The bandage almost looked worse than the wound it covered. He would certainly find her as hideous as she found herself to be.

Why had she agreed to this meeting so soon?

She needed more time—more time to heal from the accident. Surely he would understand she just got out of the hospital, wouldn't he? She moved closer to the mirror, examining the bruises that still

surrounded her eye. Though the doctor had removed the stitches because the surgical glue had held the wound closed, the bruising and redness had not gone away, and the swelling still remained. She knew she didn't want Ray to see the wound on her face until it was healed enough that she could pack a heavy layer of makeup over it.

For now, she would have to face him with the bandage on.

From the other room, she could hear muffled voices, and she worried Claudia would tell her son everything before Miriam had a chance to explain. But perhaps it would be easier for her if Claudia paved the way for her—smoothed out some of the lies she'd told. No, that wasn't fair to Claudia, who'd been just as kind to her as her son had always been.

Miriam wished she could turn back time.

Wished she'd never gotten in that buggy with Adam.

In truth, her mistakes had begun when she'd gone after Nate in a state of panic. If she'd have talked to Ray first, instead of thinking her only choice was to marry an Amish man, she might not be having to face him now in the state she was in.

Thinking back on her hasty decisions, if she'd had a trusted friend who would have sat with her while she'd waited for the results of the pregnancy test, she might not have acted out of panic. Ray was the closest thing she had to a friend. He probably would have sat there with her and waited. He would have understood. But now, he wasn't going to understand, or even concern himself with her feelings. He'd said as much when he'd caught her trying to marry Nate.

Once again, there would be no compassion for Miriam. No love. And no understanding.

She swallowed down a strangled cry as she looked into her own eyes.

Eyes that had deceived.

Eyes that had betrayed.

Eyes filled with remorse.

Unfortunately, there would also be no mercy for her now. She would have to face the consequence of her sins, and she would have to face them alone.

∽∾

A light knock sounded at Miriam's door.

She pushed at the tears that dampened her eyes and crossed to the bed. Ducking into the quilt, she pulled it over her, hoping she could convince Ray she was sleeping and he would leave her alone. Perhaps his mother had told him everything and she would never have to face him.

But that wasn't fair.

To him—or to the baby.

She had to stop thinking of herself.

Ray would certainly reject Miriam, but he wasn't the type of man to reject his own child. There was no future for her with him, but he had a future with his child, and she owed him that much.

I need to grow up, she chided herself. *I'm about to become a mamm, and I need to put this wee one first.*

She wiped her face of the evidence of defeat and pulled the covers down from her head. She sat up in the bed and breathed in deep. Ready or not, she would face Ray and get it over with.

Gott, give me strength. Put forgiveness in his heart for me, and let him accept his child.

"The door is open," Miriam said with a shaky voice.

The door opened slowly, and Ray poked his head in cautiously. When his gaze fell upon her, he rushed to the bed and sat beside her, pulling her close to him.

"I'm so glad you're okay. If I'd known you were in the hospital, I'd have come to see you sooner. I only just learned of the accident a few minutes ago."

He held her out to look at her.

She was too shocked to say anything.

He pulled her back against his shoulder.

"I know I told you I never wanted to see you again, but I didn't mean it like *that*. Please forgive me for being so harsh. Don't be angry with my mother, but she also told me about the baby, and the reason you were going to marry Nate in the first place. But what I don't understand is why you would agree to marry another Amish man instead of trusting *me* to take care of you and our baby."

Miriam couldn't answer him.

She was too busy enjoying the feel of Ray's arms around her. Oh how she loved him—still. She'd been fooling herself all this time. She couldn't go through with marrying Adam without it crushing her. She could never love Adam—she loved Ray, and would never stop. Miriam knew if she married Adam, she would forever mourn the loss of this man, whose arms she could never fall into again—not for as long as she lived.

Miriam began to cry.

Ray held her closer, stroking her hair the way he used to when she'd talk to him about missing her *mamm.* It made her feel comforted, loved, but most of all, it made her feel safe.

Why did Ray have to be so wonderful?

"I still love you, Miriam. I don't want you to marry Adam. I want you to marry *me."*

Miriam choked on her tears and hiccupped.

"Don't do this, Ray. Don't make me choose between love and responsibility to my child."

Miriam pushed away from him, realizing there was one thing Ray would never understand about her. She was Amish, and he was *Englisch,* and it would forever separate them.

CHAPTER 11

Miriam selfishly allowed Ray to hold her for some minutes before she could bring herself letting him go. She would have to tuck her feelings for him away in her heart, only to bring them out when she was most in danger of making another bad decision.

Telling herself she could only allot a portion of his love to come through for the sake of their child, was her way of dealing with the loss she would suffer. It was something she would endure for the benefit of the baby so that he or she would not have to grieve the losses she did. Miriam wished she didn't have to make such sacrifice, but she would do it for her child. She would make certain this child had the best of both worlds, no matter what it cost *her*.

Ray lifted her chin to look at her. This made her feel uncomfortable and awkward.

"I'd like to see what happened to you, Miriam. Will you remove the bandage?"

The request caught her off guard. She didn't want him to see. She didn't want anyone to see. Wasn't the humiliation of this moment bad enough without adding rejection when he looked upon her face that would forever be disfigured?

Her reluctance did not go unnoticed.

He lifted the back of his hand and stroked her other cheek, warming her skin. "I love you, Miriam, and I don't want any more secrets between us."

What did he mean by that?

He kissed her forehead ever so gently. He was the kindest man she'd ever met, and here she was rejecting *him*. He wasn't rejecting her! What was she thinking? Was it possible that she could trust this man with more than she originally thought?

She, herself, had no idea what was under the bandage at this point. She hadn't seen it for several days—the day the doctor pulled the stitches out. It was so red and puffy. She was so discouraged by her appearance that she'd let the nurses change the dressing daily, while she waited impatiently for them to cover it back up. Though a small part of her was curious, a bigger part of her didn't care if she ever looked into another mirror and looked back at the reflection.

Resorting to remaining Amish would afford her the opportunity to hide behind a mirror-less society, and she hoped in time she would forget what her own reflection looked like. After some initial shock, the community would get used to seeing the scar on her face, and she would live among a people who would never tease her for her appearance. In the *Englisch* world, she could never hide such a flawed appearance.

Giving in to Ray's gentle curiosity, Miriam tugged at the top of the bandage, peeling it slowly down her face. The white, papery tape pulled at the baby-fine hairs on her cheek, but remarkably, the wound was not as painful as it was. It had been ten days since the accident, and even her nurse had remarked at the significant healing that had taken place in such a short time. Perhaps she would be lucky, and it had miraculously healed and there would be no scar for Ray to witness.

It was a stretch, she knew.

But hope, she did.

With her wound and her dignity now exposed, Ray looked upon her with more love in his eyes than she'd ever seen in them. He tucked her close to him and kissed the side of her face near her ear.

"I still love you, Miriam. And I still want to marry you. Having a line down your face does not change things in my heart. If nothing else, it puts us more on an even playing field."

She lifted her head from his chest. "What do you mean by that?"

"I still think you're just as beautiful, but now you have been humbled by God, and you aren't so full of yourself. You used to intimidate me because you acted as if you were too good for me because of your physical beauty. You're still just as beautiful in my eyes, but actually more beautiful, because God has removed the pride in you that always stood between us."

Did he just say I was more beautiful?

"Ach, you're confusing me."

"You don't need to hide behind the Amish community for someone to love you. If you want to live in an old farmhouse with no mirrors, then that is how we will live, if it means you will accept that my love for you has *nothing* to do with how you look on the outside. I've seen what is in your heart. You've shown that part of you to me—the part you keep hidden from everyone else. You can stay in the Amish community and hide your face, but you could never hide what is in your heart—not from me."

It was as if he was looking into her very soul and plucking out her pride and tossing it aside. He was right. She had been very prideful, using her outer beauty to get what she wanted. But with Ray, she'd let her guard down and shown her heart—her *true* beauty—according to Ray. It was something she would never be able to hide from him. She had to ask herself why she would even want to.

It was a question she just couldn't answer right now.

CHAPTER 12

Miriam bandaged up her face with the gauze and tape the nurse had sent her home from the hospital with. She had survived Ray seeing the wound, and had even taken a peek at it herself when he'd left the room to greet the family that Claudia had invited to see Ray, and to meet Miriam for the first time. She was surprised at the amount of healing that had taken place in just ten short days since the accident. It had given her hope that perhaps with a small amount of makeup, she could easily hide the line down her face to where no one would see it. She would have to wait until it was completely healed though. Even so, she still wasn't ready to expose her imperfection to the world just yet.

It filled her with shame that Ray knew her so well as to call her out for her feelings of vanity over the scar on her face. He knew her well—she'd give him that much. But it wasn't enough to make her choose him over being able to hide away her imperfections in the Amish community.

Miriam adjusted her simple blue dress and checked the pins beneath her *kapp.* Soon, she would have to do away with her fancier dresses. She would miss them. But she couldn't wear them if she was a married woman in the community. Being single and in her *rumspringa* years, she could get away with a certain amount of things, but that would be all over as soon as she and Adam were wed.

She wished with all her heart that she could marry Ray. She loved Ray. It would be easy to be his *fraa.* But with Adam, it would be a lot of work to get through a lifetime in a loveless marriage.

From the other room, Miriam could hear happy chatter from a room full of women. Occasionally, a male voice would give a quick answer, but for the most part, the conversation seemed to be dominated by the women-folk.

Though Miriam was used to attending work bees and quilting bees where sometimes one hundred or more women would gather, it was within a close-knit family community. Here, the women were all strangers. She would have to learn their names, and she wasn't good in crowds of *Englischers.* But with the scar on her face, she would have a new reason to keep her eyes cast downward.

These women will be related to mei boppli, she reminded herself inwardly. *I suppose I owe it to the wee one to at least learn to know them.*

That way, when her child talked of their *aenti* or *onkel* later in life, Miriam would at least have recollection of who was being referred to.

It is what is fair to the kinner.

She stiffened her upper lip, took in a deep breath and pretended she was about to sit down to dinner with her adopted father. He was almost more of a stranger to her than the women that waited for her on the other side of the door. At least with the women that were eager to meet her, she had some sort of connection with them through Ray. Her connection to her father was lost the moment the cord of life between her and her *mamm* was severed when they put her in the ground.

Miriam opened the door slowly, and was surprised to see Ray propped against the wall outside the door.

"I was hoping you wouldn't be too much longer," he greeted her with a smile and a kiss to her cheek. "I wanted to take you in there myself so you wouldn't feel so intimidated by my aunts and cousins. They can be a bit overwhelming until you get to know them."

Miriam's feet stopped working. Maybe she wasn't ready to go in there just yet. Maybe she could be excused since she just got out of the hospital.

"I'm feeling a little tired," she said softly. "Perhaps we can do this when I've had a little more time to recover."

Ray took her gently into his arms. "You'll have to forgive my mother and my aunts, but they know you intend to marry Adam next week, and they don't think they have enough time to *talk you out of it.*"

"Talk me out of it? So that is what this dinner is all about? To bully me into changing my mind?"

Miriam was furious.

Ray held her closer. "No! I told them to back off. I told them not to say anything to you. But they think that if they are welcoming enough and shower you with love that it will make you change your mind."

He kissed her forehead. "Just go along with it for me. They really want to welcome you into our family, and it would be a shame if my family couldn't spoil you just a little. You deserve it after everything you've been through."

Miriam didn't think she deserved anything from Ray *or* his family. She'd rejected them all, but yet they were about to welcome her into their family. How would she ever be able to face them knowing she had no intention of becoming a member of their family?

"I don't know if I can deceive them like that."

"You won't be deceiving them. You don't have to become family with them to be their friend. I know you could use a few friends. Let them get to know you, so that later down the road they can tell our child they know you, and they will have good things to say about you."

Funny, *Miriam* didn't have anything good to say about herself right now.

"I will meet them. But I won't let them spoil me. It would make me feel too guilty."

Ray kissed her quickly on her lips, catching her off guard. "You won't regret this, I promise. Thank you for doing this for me. It means more than you know."

It meant a lot to her too.

She just didn't know it yet.

CHAPTER 13

Miriam looked around the room at the sea of gifts Ray's family had brought for her and the baby.

Guilt welled up in her throat, choking her.

How would she ever repay these people? They hadn't even let her help clear the table after dinner. Her debt seemed to be spiraling out of control just as her life was. If not for Ray sitting closely beside her, doting on her, she would have fainted for sure and for certain.

Embarrassed by the attention everyone was showering her with, she was grateful Ray hadn't left her side since he'd brought her out of *her* room. She wasn't used to this much attention, nor was she used to sitting around and letting others do the work that needed to be done. But they refused every offer of help she shot their way. She had not been raised to be pampered. She was raised to work hard and do whatever needed to be done until the work was finished. Unfortunately, in the Amish community, there was *always* work to be done.

Perhaps in time they will let me do my fair share of the work around here.

Between her and Ray, they had opened countless gifts that included cloth diapers, little t-shirts, bibs, toys and rattles, a silver cup, and several baby blankets and sheet sets for a crib. There were even a few envelopes boasting hefty sums of money.

The final gift, a rather large box, contained an elaborate wooden crib. It was beautiful, but it was way too fancy to use in an Amish household. It brought to Miriam's mind her own baby crib and the blankets her *mamm* had sewn for her when they'd adopted her as a newborn. It saddened her to think of the quilts her *mamm* must have spent hours sewing for her. But by marrying Adam, her *daed* would most likely let her use those things for her child. The crib had been in the family for three generations, and normally, Benjamin would have first rights to such a family heirloom, but he was as yet unattached. It was the only hope she had of getting her father to let her to use the crib.

By the time everyone went home, Miriam felt so overwhelmed, she was ready to go to bed. It wasn't that she didn't like each and every one of his family members, she was just feeling ready for some quiet-time alone to think.

Ray had other plans for her.

"I have a surprise for you," he said, taking her hands. "I was going to wait until tomorrow to show you, but I don't think I can wait that long. If we're lucky, we'll get to see it before the sun goes down completely."

Miriam fastened her seatbelt in Ray's truck, feeling the bile making its way up her throat. She swallowed hard against the acid that threatened to spill from her mouth. She'd ridden in Ray's truck plenty of times, so why was she so nervous? Perhaps it was the *surprise* he claimed he had for her. She couldn't take any more surprises right now. She needed calm and normal routines—not upheaval and surprises.

But what if it's a gut surprise?

That was likely not possible, and she knew it. Ray was too excited about this surprise for it to be anything but more pressure for her to choose him and reject Adam.

Miriam watched the flicker of the quickly-setting sun filtering through the trees as they drove down a long dirt drive toward Willow Creek. At the end of the road sat an old abandoned farm house and a barn with a collapsed roof on one side. Split-rail fencing corralled an overgrown area of land in front of the creek.

Ray parked the truck and turned to her. "We're here. What do you think?"

"The sunset over the creek is beautiful," she said warily.

"No. I mean, about the house and the barn. Isn't it great?"

She was afraid he was talking about that.

She shrugged. "For what?"

She was almost afraid to know the answer.

"For you and me to live in, that's what!"

He was way too excited about this, and Miriam couldn't think straight at all. She couldn't even respond.

"This morning, while you were sleeping, I got on the internet and started looking at property for sale. I found this piece here and it's practically *free,* it's so cheap. My dad said he would loan us the money to pay for it, and he's going to set me up with my own construction business here. I won't have to go back there and work for him anymore. I can fix up the house and the barn myself. The best part about this, is that you can remain close to the Amish community, and we can raise our child on a farm like you were raised."

Ray looked at Miriam, who, by this time, had tears in her eyes. But they were not happy tears. They were tears of remorse. Tears of regret.

"Aren't you going to say something?" he asked softly.

"I wish it was that simple," she said, hiccupping.

Ray hopped out of the truck and jogged around to her side and opened the door.

He held his hand out to her and she took it reluctantly. "Let me show you," he said with a smile.

She could not resist that smile.

They walked up onto the front porch of the white-washed, clapboard house that boasted a rickety porch swing.

Ray pointed to the swing. "I can fix that. Imagine how many summer nights we would enjoy out here sipping lemonade and rocking the baby to sleep."

Tears ran down Miriam's face.

She could see it.

They walked in the through the broken front door and into the front room with dirty wooden floors and a brick fireplace on the far wall between two broken windows.

"I'll fix the door so it closes—and locks, so you'll feel safe. I can put in new windows, of course. You could make pretty curtains and make braided rugs for the hardwood floors. The upstairs has four bedrooms. And the kitchen—the kitchen has a huge pantry for all the canning jars I know you'll fill it with. Can you see us living here, Darlin'?"

Miriam could see it.

And that's what scared her the most.

CHAPTER 14

Miriam found a note from Claudia addressed to her sitting on the kitchen counter next to a large paper sack with handles. The letter stated she would be home early from the store, and that the bag contained all the items she would need to get her started on her new venture. The letter also boasted that Claudia had another idea to help her out, and that it was a surprise.

Miriam didn't think she could stomach anymore surprises. But her curiosity got the better of her. She peeked inside the large shopping bag to find all the materials she needed to make at least one hundred Amish dolls.

Finally, something I can do to start paying my way around here.

Miriam took the bag and her cup of coffee back to her room and laid it out on the bed to begin. As she started to cut the pattern she'd memorized when she was only a child, she realized she had no wedding dress in which to marry Adam. She didn't dare ask Claudia or Ray for such a thing, but perhaps she could ask her brother to get her some material to make one when he arrived for his visit on Friday. That wouldn't leave her much time to do the sewing, but perhaps she could wear her navy blue dress and make only a new pinafore for the wedding.

Her own wedding dress had been left at the B&B, and even if recovered, was swathed in chicken guts. The blood would not come out of the garment after this much time had passed. The dress she'd taken from Levinia was not recovered from the remains of the accident. And so she was left with no other choice than to wear the plain, navy blue dress, unless she could talk her brother into providing her with enough money to get the material for a new pinafore.

For now, Miriam was content to make as many Amish dolls as Claudia's store could carry. Miriam was desperate for the money to pay back Bethany. It could mean the difference between her acceptance back into the community once she and Adam had the Bishop publish their wedding. A full confession would be required of her. She was, indeed, prepared to give the confession she should have given the day of the accident. She would do that on Sunday when she attended services with Adam and Benjamin.

Miriam began to sew the pieces together to make her first doll. She pondered the events of the past two weeks, wondering if things might have been different if she'd have just given the confession that was expected of her that day. What had she been thinking? She supposed she was thinking the same thing she believed now, but only then, she acted in haste.

Was she still acting in haste? Was she making the best decision she could for her and her child? Her own feelings couldn't be an issue anymore. She had to grow up and put her child first. But would that child understand having a stepfather in his or her life instead of a real father. She had not had her real father or mother in her life, and it was something she'd always craved, despite the love her *mamm* had showered her with.

It wasn't the same as the situation with her birth parents. At least her child would know his or her real father, unlike Miriam had. No, Miriam would make certain her child knew its real father no matter how hard it would be for her to never be able to live her life with Ray. She hoped that in time it would be easier for her to be around him. But now, in her current state, the pregnancy made her feel vulnerable and needy.

Truth be told, she wished there was another way, but she just wasn't brave enough to stand alone away from the only family she'd ever known. Perhaps with *grandkinner,* her *daed* would come around a little more, and she and Adam would have the support of his Amish community to help set up their life together as a married couple.

It was the perfect plan.

So why did everything about it seem so wrong?

Perhaps it was the love she still carried for Ray that was clouding her judgment. She knew she needed to ignore those feelings in order to stay on course. It would be difficult to ignore with him in the same house for the next few days until her wedding, but she would have to find a way to steer clear of him as best she could. And though he expected a final answer about the house, she'd tried her best to let him down easy and he hadn't taken the hint.

Unfortunate for her, there was no more time for subtlety. She would have to break Ray's heart all over again, and that nearly broke her spirit to even think about it. He needed to know she intended to go through with marrying Adam, no matter what.

She prayed he would understand, and that the hurt would be minimal—to both of them.

Lord, take away the love Ray has for me. Give him understanding and wisdom to accept my decision about marrying Adam. Take away the love I have for Ray and please stop my heart from breaking.

Miriam stifled a sob, but she couldn't prevent the tears from pouring down her cheeks.

If it be Your Wille, Gott, she added.

CHAPTER 15

Miriam stumbled sleepily into the kitchen, hoping to find some fresh coffee. She could smell it, but worried there wouldn't be any left since she'd gotten up late. She'd tossed and turned so much during the night over all the stress of Ray's announcement last night, that she hadn't fallen asleep until nearly four-thirty this morning.

Now noon, she was certain she would be alone in the house. Claudia would be at her store, and Ray was surely busy setting up his new business his father had promised to help him with. She shuffled up to the counter and pulled a clean coffee cup from the cupboard and held it under the spout on the coffee-maker. Fresh, *hot* coffee drained into her cup while her heart did a somersault behind her ribcage. If there was hot coffee, someone was home besides her. Looking up, she spotted Ray sitting at the small table just off the kitchen sipping a steaming cup.

I should have stayed in my room, she grumbled to herself.

"I was hoping you'd get up while I was here getting a little lunch. I've already put in a full day's work, but I suppose you probably had a little trouble sleeping last night with all the excitement of yesterday."

Miriam forced a smile, but quickly let it go when the expression cinched her wound. Her hand instinctively went up to her cheek, holding the bandage against the tightness. She wondered if she would ever be able to really smile again—but not just because she worried about breaching her wound. A sadness filled her at the sight of Ray, knowing that marrying Adam would never be able to fill that void in her heart.

He rushed to her side. "Are you in pain?"

She shook her head, unable to look at him without worrying she would cry.

"Are you ill? My mother told me you would probably get sick a lot in the beginning of your pregnancy."

She shook her head again, hoping she could convince him. She knew if she let on how she was feeling, he would take her in his strong arms, and she would be powerless to escape his loving embrace.

She wanted to be his *fraa,* but that just wasn't possible. But she could allow him to hold her, couldn't she? No, that could be too risky. She would never want to give him up, but she *had* to.

Lord, please give me the strength to resist this mann's love.

He closed the space between them, causing her to take an instinctive step backward.

"Come here, Darlin', and let me hold you. You're shaking."

She clenched her jaw to keep her teeth from chattering. Her nerves were causing bile to form in her throat. Her willfulness was ineffective against his persistence. He had her in his arms before she could put up her defenses. This was where she wanted to be; it was where she was meant to be. But she couldn't—could she? Should she?

His mouth found her neck as he leaned down to deepen the hug. Sweet kisses tickled her neck as he swept his lips over her jawline and to her cheek, where they suddenly consumed her mouth. Giving in to his passion, Miriam couldn't help but deepen the kiss. She couldn't stop herself. She wanted him for a husband in every way. She wanted to raise their child with him. She even wanted that *happily ever after* with him.

Reality made her heart skip a beat.

It made her throat constrict with tears.

If she didn't push him away, the reality would surely suffocate her.

It would pull her further down into the depression she'd settled into.

With a gentle nudge, Miriam separated from him. Her eyes closed, and her breathing came in jagged gasps.

"What's wrong, Darlin'?" Ray asked.

She held her hands up in front of her, eyes still closed. "I—can't."

She felt him making a subtle attempt at pulling her back into his arms, but she remained too rigid for him to embrace her without force.

"I want us to be a family, Miriam. That's why I went ahead and purchased that farm on Willow Creek this morning."

Her eyes flung open, and she stared him down.

"You did what?"

"My dad went with me this morning and he paid cash for the farm. He wrote up a mortgage for me to take over. I've been over there for two hours already taking inventory of all the supplies we need to fix the place up."

He looked at Miriam, who stared blankly at him.

"Well, aren't you going to say something?"

She hiccupped as she tried to pull in a deep breath. "You shouldn't have bought that place. Not for me. Not for *us*. I'm still planning on marrying Adam."

His face drained of all color.

"*Why?*" he asked, barely above a whisper.

"I *must.*"

Ray clutched her arms gently, desperation in his eyes. "But you just kissed me! I thought you— loved me."

She didn't dare admit her love for him. If she did, he would never let her go, and he had to. She needed him to release her from the guilt that plagued her. The guilt had taken up residence in her mind, embedding itself like a nightmare.

Who was she kidding?

This *was* certainly a nightmare, and one she couldn't wake up from.

"I still intend on marrying Adam. Please don't make me say it again. He will be taking me to Sunday service, and our wedding will be published then."

"If you think I'm going to stand by and let you marry another Amish man, then you don't know me at all."

Miriam narrowed her gaze on Ray.

"Another Amish man? I didn't marry the first one—but I *will* be marrying this one—and you won't be able to stand in my way. My mind is made up."

"Then change it, because I'm not letting you go," he said as he stormed out of the kitchen door.

Miriam watched him tuck his head against the wind as he walked out toward the wooded area behind his mother's house. She was momentarily tempted to take him his coat, which he'd left on the hook by the door, but she decided it was best to let him *cool off.*

CHAPTER 16

Miriam wiped a fresh tear to keep it from soiling the doll she was stitching by hand. Sewing the dolls was just what she needed to keep her idle hands busy until she recovered from the accident, but there was nothing that could keep her idle thoughts from turning to Ray. They'd had an argument, and Miriam had reasoned with herself now more than ever that it was simply not meant to be between the two of them.

The sound of buggy wheels grinding against the concrete driveway, and the hollow sound of the horse's steady, clip-clop as it drew nearer to the house, startled her from her depressing thoughts. She peered out the blinds to see Adam pulling his horse into the circle driveway.

Her heart thumped hard and fast. Not with excitement over her betrothed, but with dread. The kind of dread that fills you with the deepest form of regret and shame, it's too unbearable to live with.

Adam wasn't supposed to come for her until Sunday. Today was Wednesday. What could he possibly be doing here so soon?

Her first instinct was to go back to her room and not answer the door, but she knew she had to face him sooner or later. Best to get it over with so she could go about the business of making the dolls to pay back her debt to Bethany, and put aside a little for the baby. She couldn't afford the interruption right now, but this was all part of her growing up and taking responsibility for the mistakes she'd made.

Miriam jumped as the footfalls on the porch concluded with a ring to the doorbell. It startled her, as she was not used to hearing the sound of the *Englischer* device. It struck her as odd that Adam would ring the doorbell instead of knocking, but, perhaps he might think someone was home with her. Was it possible that he knew Ray was here?

A new thought occurred to her.

Worry suddenly flooded her thoughts as she wondered what would happen if Ray were to intercept Adam's visit and show his disapproval. She supposed it was an inevitable happenstance, but that didn't mean she wouldn't avoid the opportunity at all cost.

Miriam lifted her still-aching body from the leather recliner and went to the door before the bell rang a second time. She pasted a smile on her face and swung open the door as if she was happy to see Adam. No sense in giving him a reason to back out of marrying her.

"*Gudemariye,*" she said just the way her *mamm* had taught her when she was little. Miriam had, for the most part, spoken as an *Englischer* ever since her *mamm's* funeral, making every effort to lose her accent. It had been what had separated her from her adopted father and brother—her unwillingness to adhere to the Amish way of life.

Now, as she spoke to Adam, she intended to prove she would make a smart match for him in every way—right down to carrying on the use of their language to child she now carried, and any future *kinner* she would bear for him.

She felt suddenly dizzy and sick to her stomach at the thought of having the same intimate relationship she'd had with Ray. She couldn't imagine being that submissive to anyone other than Ray, whom she loved.

Adam leaned in and awkwardly kissed her forehead. It happened so quickly she didn't have time to react.

"Do you think you might be up to a buggy ride?"

Her heart quickened its pace and her cheeks flushed. She wasn't ready, but she supposed she had to start trusting him at some point. After all, he was to be her husband in only a few short days.

"*Jah,*" she said, suddenly feeling very *fake*.

"Where would you like to go?"

Miriam didn't have to think about it. If she was to remain in this community as Adam's *fraa,* there would be a lot of fences for her to mend. She would have to start with the hardest one—Bethany. She not only owed her an apology, she would have to settle her debt with the girl before she made her confession to the Bishop prior to the wedding.

After voicing her destination to Adam, they were on their way down the long driveway to the main road that led back to Willow Creek. She occupied her mind with the layout of the house Ray had bought for the two of them to pass the time it took to travel, and to keep her mind from getting anxious over being in Adam's buggy again.

In her mind's eye, she mentally furnished the home, while Ray started a crackling fire, where she would sit in the hand-carved rocking chair with their baby at her breast. It was only a dream, but it was a good dream—one that she shared with Ray.

But here she was, sitting beside Adam—her betrothed, thinking of Ray tinkering around the home he would fix up just for the three of them.

The three of them.

It had a nice sound to it. She could see him cuddling and cooing their baby, and then handing him or her back to its *mamm—her!*

No matter how many times she told herself, she still couldn't comprehend what it would be like to be a *mamm.* Claudia told her it would happen in an instant the first time she held the wee one, but she worried she lacked the natural instincts to care for a child. She was already convinced Ray would love their child, and she knew she had the same love in her heart, but she'd been raised by two men, and they weren't exactly the mothering types.

"We're here," Adam announced.

Miriam reluctantly let go of her daydream, ready to face the reality that had become her life.

CHAPTER 17

Miriam's heart drummed against her ribcage at the sight of the B&B. How had they gotten there so soon? She wasn't ready for what she was about to do, but she took a deep breath and stepped out of the buggy regardless. Her shaky legs refused to take her any further until Adam slipped his arm around her shoulder and gently guided her toward the house. Her first instinct was to shrug him off, but she was so shaky, she feared she might faint if not for his hold on her. It made her feel like an invalid, but she didn't care at the moment. Her only concern was how she would broach the subject of her debt with Bethany.

The front door swung open as she approached the porch, and Bethany stood there with a smug look on her face. Though she knew she deserved nothing less from Bethany, Miriam felt the sting of her disdain.

"I came to apologize," Miriam immediately offered.

Bethany posted her fists on her hips. "I should think so after everything you did to hurt *mei schweschder* and me."

You forgot to say how I deserve everything that's happened to me, Miriam thought.

"I'm truly sorry for what I did, and I wanted you to know I intend to pay back every bit of the money I took from you."

Bethany looked at Miriam to see if she detected truthfulness. She couldn't tell. "You mean, poor Adam, here, is going to have to pay back your debt after he marries you!"

"*Nee,*" Miriam said holding out a finished doll she held in her hands. "I'm making these for a store downtown that Ray's mother owns. She's letting me sell them and keep the profits."

Bethany examined the doll's fine stitching.

"How long do you think that will last after you marry Adam instead of Ray?"

"The offer was not conditional," Miriam said defensively. "It is for the *boppli,* not for me."

Bethany skewed her mouth. "I hope you're right."

Miriam pursed her lips, but held her tongue.

"I came to say my peace, and to give this to Levinia. I don't imagine she is here anymore as she's married now, but would you give it to her with my apology?"

Bethany took the doll. "I'll give her the doll, but I think the apology should come from you."

Miriam nodded agreement. *"Danki."*

She looped her arm in the crook of Adam's elbow and allowed him to assist her down the stairs of the large, wraparound porch, and into his buggy. It was there that she realized just how long of a road it was going to be before the members of the community accepted her again. She'd really messed things up for herself here, but she hoped to redeem herself with her change in attitude, and the true remorse she held in her heart.

∂∘≪

A knock at the door startled Miriam. She'd fallen asleep in the recliner with a half-sewn doll in her hands and hadn't heard anyone approach the house. The afternoon spent with Adam had stressed her out so much she'd worn herself out with worry. He'd been kind to her, and a perfect gentleman, but that was exactly the problem. He'd been so nice it had caused more guilt to build up in her over marrying him.

Miriam forced herself out of the recliner to answer the door, though she was in no mood to see anyone. But since it was Claudia's home, she figured that as a guest, she'd better see to the door in case it was something or someone important.

Surprise filled Miriam at the sight of Levinia standing on the porch, her blue wedding dress draped over her arms.

Levinia held the dress out to her. "I thought you might need this for your wedding. I cleaned it for you. There isn't a trace of mess after what *mei schweschder* did to it. Bethany gave me the doll you sewed for me. *Danki.* I'm certain you will make a fair amount of money selling them. Your stitching is very *gut.*

Bethany asked me to tell you that she doesn't expect the money to be returned to her all at once. You can take your time in paying her back a little at a time. We know you need the money for your *boppli,* and Bethany has changed her mind about getting a car with the money—after what *happened.* We are both very sorry for what happened to you."

A lump formed in Miriam's throat. She didn't deserve such kindness from either of them, but they had both extended it nonetheless.

"Won't you come in for some tea?" Miriam asked, opening the door fully and stepping back to let her first *guest* in.

"Danki."

Levinia followed her into the kitchen after Miriam set her clean dress down on the sofa in the living room. She would fix her guest some tea, and hope to make amends with her. She knew they would probably never be friends, but they would be neighbors, and reside in the same community. Their *kinner* would be cousins, and for that reason alone, perhaps, just maybe, Levinia might learn to forgive her eventually. For now, she would understand that the clean dress presented to her was a peace offering.

While Miriam and Levinia sipped tea and nibbled on fresh-baked cookies, they discovered they had just a bit more in common than they could have ever imagined. Miriam was surprised to hear that she and Bethany had also grown up without their *mamm.* Seeing how well-adjusted they were compared to her, Miriam decided that the two of them might just be a good example to her. They whiled away the afternoon with tales of mischief from their youth, and even shared a few laughs. It was refreshing to Miriam to see that life did not have to be so difficult. That perhaps there *was* a chance they could someday be *gut* friends.

CHAPTER 18

Miriam woke early feeling heavier at heart than she had ever felt in her life—even after her *mamm* had died. Her conscience bothered her about too many things to sleep. The house was quiet—too quiet. At least at her own home, she had chickens that would be clucking, roosters crowing and cows bellowing—all for their morning meal. Here, she had no one to care for, no one to rise for, and no one to feed—yet.

She rolled her hand over the small of her abdomen. She would be showing soon—too soon. Everyone in the community would know she was with child—if they didn't already. She wasn't certain how long a pregnancy could be hidden, especially after the gossip that had circulated about one of the girls she'd gone to school with. They weren't friends, but she'd heard she'd become pregnant before her wedding. It was all the youth in the community talked about.

Miriam wondered if *she* was being talked about the same way in this community, and if the members of her own community already knew. The gossip-mill among the Amish could be pretty harsh at times. When someone in the community committed a sin, everyone knew. As long as there was a confession, there was forgiveness among the people, but she would forever be *used* as an example to the other youth.

Forever talked about.

Forever reminded of the sins of her youth.

Would it be the same among the *Englisch?*

Miriam could no longer take the silence that drove her thoughts. She *had* to get up—even if it disturbed Ray and Claudia. She *had* to do something besides lying here awake to contend with her thoughts. She needed to occupy her mind. Though she had several dolls already sewn, and more yet to be sewn, she needed something a little more challenging to do this morning.

Perhaps she could prepare the morning meal for the household. But Claudia had a modern stove that Miriam had no idea how to operate. Besides, it was still too early. The sun hadn't even made its appearance on the horizon yet, and no birds chirped in the trees outside her window.

All was asleep, and all was quiet.

She rose from the bed anyway and quickly made it up, pulling the fancy quilt over the ruffled sheets. She liked the modern things, but it wasn't something she should get used to if she was to be an Amish *fraa*. Marrying among the Amish meant primitive belongings and hard work from sun-up to sundown, and beyond that if there were *kinner* in the *haus*. Would Claudia be willing to relieve some of the burden of raising the *boppli* from her? She hoped it was so, even though she would be married to Adam.

In the kitchen, she surprisingly found the ingredients she needed to make bread. Locating glass loaf pans that seemed too clean to have ever been used, she set them on the counter with the rest of the stuff she'd gathered from Claudia's pantry. She went about mixing and stirring, occupying her mind from her troubles.

When Miriam was young, her *mamm* had taught her that making bread was the best way to solve almost any problem. In the time it took to prepare, most things could be worked out. And the kneading of the dough was not only *gut* for working out frustrations, it was *gut* for making the arms strong enough to do other chores.

Miriam had no idea if what her *mamm* told her was true, but simply being reminded of her soothed her more than she could have thought. Usually, thinking of her *mamm* had always filled her with bittersweet memories that made her heart ache, but at this moment, for some reason beyond her reasoning, it brought her comfort.

Hearing a faint noise, Miriam looked over her shoulder to find Claudia entering the kitchen. Her fluffy robe was tied in a knot at her waste, and she lifted a hand to rub the sleep from her blue eyes that matched Ray's.

"I'm sorry if I made too much noise and woke you," Miriam immediately offered.

Claudia waved a hand at her. "No worries. I have to do inventory at the store today, and I had to be up early."

Miriam glanced at the clock on the wall and made note that the window above the sink still hadn't illuminated any hint of the sun.

"Surely not *this* early. But if you wouldn't mind helping me figure out how to turn on your oven, I'd be ever so grateful."

Claudia chuckled. "By the looks of things, I'd say you had trouble sleeping."

"*Jah*—yes."

Claudia crossed to the stove and pushed a few buttons causing a series of beeps. "It's on. When you want it off, just push this button."

"*Danki*—thank you."

Miriam didn't know why she was reverting to speaking as she'd been taught in her growing years, but she supposed it was because of her uncertainty as to where she fit in. She was between worlds, and had no idea which she preferred at the moment.

Claudia moved to the coffee maker and began to make a fresh pot. Miriam was grateful for that. She was in need of a cup to soothe her shakes, and she had no idea how to operate the modern device.

"I remember when I was first pregnant with Ray, and how terrified I was. I didn't sleep much the entire pregnancy, come to think of it. But trust me when I say, you should get your sleep now, because once that little one is born, you won't get much sleep for the first few years of its life."

Miriam gulped down a lump of fear that suddenly entered her throat. "Years?"

Claudia cupped an arm around Miriam's shoulder and gave her a quick squeeze before returning to the chore of making coffee. "I didn't mean to frighten you. I didn't have my mother around to help me, or give me advice about mothering. The trick is to sleep when they sleep. If you don't, you'll be exhausted. But I will be there if you need anything, whether it be advice like that, or just to help care for the baby if you get overwhelmed."

"Even if I don't marry Ray?" she asked cautiously.

Claudia smiled. "Even if you don't marry Ray."

Miriam felt a burden lift from her as she kneaded the bread dough. Her *mamm* had been right. Making bread can help you work out a multitude of problems.

CHAPTER 19

Miriam pulled the dressing from her cheek and examined it in the bathroom mirror. Surprised at how much it had healed, she felt a little foolish for keeping the bandage on it for so long. The nurse at the hospital had given her instructions before leaving that stated she would only have to wear the bandage for a few days after leaving.

That time had since passed.

She quickly re-dressed the wound and went back to the kitchen, where dishes awaited her attention. She ran her hand along the bandage, wondering if she would ever feel it was ready to remain uncovered.

Part of her had kept it covered from Ray's view, even though he'd made such a fuss about telling her it didn't disgust him the way it did her. Mostly, she'd kept it hidden from herself. She didn't relish the idea of catching a glimpse of her scarred face every time she passed one of the many mirrors in Claudia's home. The majority of Amish homes didn't contain even one mirror. She would make certain that there were none in the home she would share with Adam. She didn't want the constant reminder that she was less than perfect.

Now, the wound was a mere, pink line down her face that she thought could easily be covered with makeup. But she would not be living among the *Englisch* where such a thing was commonplace, and even acceptable. Among the Amish, worrying about outer beauty was considered a sin of vanity.

Miriam had been guilty of vanity most of her life. From the time she was very young, she knew she didn't look like any of her cousins, and was said to be much prettier than they were. It was talked about in hushed tones, but she was always aware of the chatter.

The girls in school had mistreated her out of jealousy, and it had turned Miriam bitter toward them, causing her difficulty in making friends. Because of this, she'd turned to seeking the attention from the boys, causing even more strife with her female competitors.

They wouldn't be jealous of me now, she thought.

In her opinion, being unwed and pregnant with a scar on her face qualified her for a little sympathy. But she wasn't looking to be pitied; she wanted acceptance. Ray's cousins and *aenti's* had certainly accepted her. She wondered, though, if it had been genuine, or if they had been kind only because she carried Ray's *kinner*.

Miriam finished wiping down the kitchen and putting away the rest of the morning meal, including the bread she'd baked, when Ray entered the room. He approached her from behind, catching her off-guard, tucking his face in her neck and slipping his arm over her abdomen.

"How are my two favorite people this morning?"

He made her feel a little awkward, but in a good way. She loved the gentle attention he showered her with, as though she was the most cherished thing in his life.

"You sound like you had a better night's sleep than I did."

He kissed her lightly and crossed to the coffee maker to dispense a single cup from the reservoir.

The warmth of his kiss remained on her neck, causing her to miss the contact between them. She knew it was wrong to accept the attention from him since she was promised to marry Adam, but she reasoned with herself it was acceptable since she was carrying Ray's child. She was so confused about her feelings she didn't trust herself to make the right decision at all. Most of her time, lately, consisted of arguing with herself as to whether or not she was making the right choice. One minute she would think it was a solid, sane option, and the next, Ray would do something to make her doubt her selection, as he'd just done.

"I *did* sleep like a bear hibernating in the winter, but probably because of all the hard work I've put into our house for the last couple of days."

Miriam cringed at his comment to include *her* in the ownership of the house he'd purchased. She wasn't certain if he was *trying* to put pressure on her and fill her with guilt about marrying Adam, but he couldn't possibly add to the amount she'd already piled on herself.

Ray sat at the table and sipped his steaming coffee. Claudia had left more than a half hour before, but the coffee she'd made had remained hot in the automated warmer.

"Would you like something to eat?"

Ray sniffed the air. "Whatever you made smells heavenly, and I'm starving."

Miriam removed the plate from the refrigerator that she'd just put away for him, and put it in the microwave. She pushed the buttons just like Claudia had taught her only a few short minutes before she'd left for the day, and told her it was "*Just in case my son wakes up and wants to sample your wonderful cooking.*" She'd winked at her and told her, "*The way to a man's heart is through his stomach.*"

But Miriam wasn't looking to win Ray's heart. She already had it, and she was throwing it away like a fool. It was another wrong in her life she would have to learn to accept.

As she placed the food in front of Ray, she took pleasure in watching him as he dipped his face toward the steaming plate and breathed in the aroma with a smile spread wide across his full lips. She could get used to spending her days cooking for him and submitting to him in every way.

He was easy to love, and leaving him was going to be the hardest thing she would ever have to do.

The clip-clop of a horse approaching broke the spell between them, sending Miriam's thoughts into sudden turmoil.

"I think your *boyfriend* is here," Ray muttered under his breath as he glared out the kitchen window.

Miriam didn't blame him for being upset, but his comment stung.

"He isn't my *boyfriend,*" she snapped.

Ray stood up and took his empty plate to the sink, letting it drop haphazardly.

"You're right. He's your fiancé—your *betrothed,* as *you* would say."

"Ray, please don't…"

"Don't what? You're carrying *my* baby, and I love you! Help me to understand why you're marrying *him?*"

Miriam stifled a sob that threatened to shake her vocal chords. "I don't expect you to *ever* understand, but if you really love me, you'll accept it."

"You're right about one thing. I'll *never* understand, but I won't *ever* accept it either." He walked outside and greeted Adam briefly as he shouldered past him to the unattached garage.

Miriam threw her shawl over her shoulders and went out to meet Adam. His timing couldn't have been worse, but she hoped that perhaps his appearance would help Ray to come to terms with the reality of her impending marriage. Only problem was, she, herself, needed convincing of the reality too.

"*Gudemariye,* Miriam," Adam said cheerfully.

It nauseated her to hear that from him. Only a few short moments before, it had been music to her ears to hear Ray's smooth baritone say the same thing to her—but only in *Englisch.*

"Good morning, Adam," she said sternly. "What are you doing here? I wasn't expecting you until Sunday for the service. My brother, Benjamin will be here tomorrow to tend to my needs, so you shouldn't have come all this way for nothing."

"You're sounding more and more like an *Englischer* the more I speak to you," he said impatiently. "As long as you don't talk that way once we are married, so as not to shame me within the community."

Miriam placed her hands on her hips defensively. "Shame you? In case you've forgotten, I *am* an *Englischer.*"

"*Jah,* but you were raised Amish. And I pray that you will raise our *kinner* in the Amish ways, and teach them the language of our community."

Miriam narrowed her eyes at Adam. "First of all, this *baby* is *mine*—not *ours.* And second, I wasn't planning on having any more children, so you won't have any children of your own."

Adam's expression fell. "Perhaps you misunderstood me when I offered to marry you that I would be raising *your boppli* as my own."

"Let's not forget that you *offered* to marry me as penance for the accident you caused; I only agreed to marry you as a matter of convenience."

"Convenience?" he asked.

"Surely you don't think I could ever *love* you!"

Adam lowered his head, defeat shadowing his expression. "My offer to you was genuine. I intend to make an effort to love you, and I hoped you would do the same for me. I intended to be a *gut* husband to you."

"I don't need you to love me. All I need is your good name and your Amish heritage. Let's just leave it at that."

Adam removed his straw hat, revealing tightly-coiled, flaxen curls. Funny that she'd never really taken the time to look at him or get to know him. He was very handsome, and kind as could be, but would those things be enough to make her forget Ray? Suddenly she noticed the sadness in his blue-green eyes, his height and strength no longer able to carry the weight of the burden she'd put on his broad shoulders.

"I'm determined to make it work, even if you're not," he said. "Perhaps you should consider moving into the B&B until we are wed."

"Why would I do that?" she shrieked. "I'm perfectly happy here."

"I'm not certain that being around the *vadder* of your *boppli* is such a *gut* idea…"

"Ray is my baby's father," she interrupted. "He will *always* be the baby's father, and he will *always* be a part of *my* child's life, so you'd better get used to his presence in our lives now."

Adam cleared his throat nervously. He was no match for Miriam's fury where the *boppli* was concerned, and she could see it in his posture. But she couldn't take back what she'd said to him. It was the truth and it needed to be said now, before it was too late.

"I was hoping that he would only want to see the *boppli* once for his peace of mind, and then allow you and me to do the raising—in the Amish ways. If that is not how it will be, perhaps I will have to discuss it with Ray instead."

Miriam pursed her lips. "We have already discussed it, and I *told* you how it was going to be. Either accept it, or…"

She let her voice trail off. She didn't want to finish the sentence. Didn't want to give him and *out.* She needed him to marry her, but she also felt it was important that Adam understood she couldn't let Ray go—even if she was married to *him.*

"I will be here to pick you up on Sunday for the service. The Bishop is still requiring a confession from you that you never gave, and he's expecting one from me now."

Miriam pointed to the bandage on her face.

"You mean for this? I should hope so!"

She stormed off, knowing how unfair she was being to him, but she just couldn't look him in the eye another minute. Her harsh words crushed him, and she worried that he would now back out of their arrangement.

She secretly wondered if she didn't hope he would.

CHAPTER 20

Ray walked in through the kitchen, determined to catch Miriam before she had a chance to hide herself away in her room. After overhearing the heated argument between her and Adam, he deemed this to be his best chance to change her mind before things got so far out of control there would be no fixing it.

She would be vulnerable now, and emotional, so he knew he would have to treat her with an extra dose of patience and love. But he wouldn't pass up such an opportunity to salvage his family and his future with the woman he loved more than his own life.

His heart sank when he didn't find her in the kitchen, but muffled weeping told him he would find her in her bedroom. As he rounded the corner of the living room, the crying reached his ears at the level that let him know she hadn't bothered to close the bedroom door.

Thankfully, his hopeful assumption was correct.

He stood quietly in the doorway for a moment, watching her shoulders shake as she cried into one of the overstuffed pillows that decorated the bed. His first instinct was to go to her, but he wasn't sure he should risk pushing her to the point she rejected his comfort.

Deciding it was worth the risk, he closed the space between them and slipped down onto the edge of the bed next to her and gently pulled her into his arms. She buried her face against his shoulder and trembled as she let loose heartbreaking cries. He had no idea what she was going through. He only knew he loved her and would do anything to help her.

Disheartened by her sobbing, he smoothed her soft, golden hair, burying his face in the sleek tendrils scented with honeysuckle flowers. He'd missed the fragrance of the homemade soap she used on her hair that yielded the silky feel of it between his fingers.

"Everything is going to be alright, Darlin'. You'll see things aren't as bad as they seem right now."

"They…are that bad," she managed in-between sobs catching in her throat. "And they're only going to get worse."

He ran his hand down the length of her hair, which she'd let loose from the tightly-wound bun at the base of her neck.

"I doesn't have to be," he said cautiously. "Marry *me,* and let me fix this for you."

"You can't fix this any more than I can," she managed with one breath. "I'm beginning to think it isn't going to matter if I marry either of you."

He kissed the top of her head, breathing in the aromatic bouquet.

Lord, help me convince Miriam that I love her, he prayed silently. *Give her the strength to accept my help. Forgive us for the sins we committed, and bless us with the opportunity to make it right by getting married.*

He wasn't sure if God had heard him, but he prayed it with all his heart nonetheless. It had been a while since he'd talked to God. He hadn't exactly walked the straight and narrow path with Miriam. His heart weighed heavy with the guilt of the situation he'd put her in. He was determined to spend the rest of his days making things right with her, but it wasn't going to be easy if she continued to resist his efforts.

"I'm sorry for the things I said to you earlier," he said thoughtfully. "The last thing I want to do is add to the pressure you must already feel."

Miriam lifted her head from his shoulder. Though her eyes were red and puffy from crying, he thought she'd never looked more beautiful. He tucked his hand under her chin and lifted while he bent down enough to touch his lips to hers. He couldn't help himself. He loved her, and he wanted her to know it.

He wanted her to trust his love, and to trust *him*.

Delight filled him as she deepened the kiss between them. He held her like it was the last time he would ever be able to. He feared it would be, but he savored this moment and the sweetness of her lips as they swept across his. He wanted to love her for the rest of his life—if only she would let him.

She pushed away from him all too soon.

"This isn't such a *gut* idea," she managed, breathlessly. "I'm betraying my betrothed."

Ray jumped up from where he sat beside her.

"Betraying *him?* You will betray *me* if you marry him!"

She shook her head without looking at him.

"If you can look me in the eye and tell me you don't love me, then I will step aside and let you marry him."

Ray knew it was a risky ultimatum, but he had to know once and for all where he stood.

She remained silent, and he could see the pain in her eyes as she began to weep.

"You can't tell me," he said softly. "Because you still love me. At least you kissed me just now like you did. That wasn't a casual kiss—that was a kiss filled with love. It left me wanting, and I believe it did the same for you."

"I *have* to marry Adam," she managed in between sobs.

"You don't have to! You can marry me, but it seems you are too much of a coward to do what's right."

He knew his words were harsh, but he simply had no more words for her.

CHAPTER 21

Miriam shivered as she strolled into the kitchen. The thick robe Claudia had given her was wrapped tightly around her, but it wasn't keeping in her body heat. She hoped that a cup of hot tea would warm her enough to get some rest. It was already late, and she just couldn't get warm enough to relax, let alone, to fall asleep. The fancy quilt on her bed was made more for decoration than practical use. The quilts back home did their job to keep a body warm, even on the coldest of winter nights. Right now, she missed them more than ever.

She shivered again as she looked out the kitchen window at the light flurries swirling about in the lamplight just outside the window. The decorative light-post illuminated the flakes of snow, causing her to feel a chill to the bone. Winter was going to be rough if it was already snowing. November had only just begun.

From the cupboard, Miriam pulled out a teacup and the box of chamomile tea. She filled the tea kettle and lit the stubborn burner on the gas stove from the box of matches Claudia kept in a primitive tin canister on the counter. It reminded her of the sort of wares she might find in an Amish kitchen. Claudia's entire décor was country and antiques. It was a comfortable old farm house, and Miriam thought it to be not too much unlike her own family home.

A noise from the family room startled her. Miriam followed the noise, finding Ray at the hearth putting thick wedges of wood in a stack on the fireplace grate.

He looked up and smiled warmly when she entered the room. "I heard you walk past my room, and figured you were cold, so I came out here to start a fire to warm you up."

He already knows me too well.

Miriam swooned at the gesture. He was the kindest man she'd ever met, and it filled her with guilt that he was kind to her, despite her constantly rejecting him.

"*Danki,*" she said quietly. "It's snowing—come see out the kitchen window."

He followed her into the kitchen and stood behind her at the window above the sink. He wrapped both his arms around her, holding her close and tucking his face in her neck. She allowed him to hold her as they stared out the window at the snow that fluttered around whimsically, as if perfectly choreographed for an encore performance for their eyes only.

The whistle of the tea kettle caused Miriam to jump. Feeling suddenly awkward, Ray let her slip out of his arms and excused himself to finish building the fire in the other room.

Miriam pulled another teacup from the cupboard, still feeling the warmth of Ray's arms around her. It instilled in her a desire to return the kindness he'd shown her by serving him some hot tea. It was the least she could do for him after the way she'd treated him earlier.

Miriam longed to care for Ray in the manner that a wife would, but she couldn't. She wished he could understand how much she would always care for him despite the fact she would be marrying another man, but it was not something that would likely come to pass. There would most likely always be strife between them as they tried to raise their child together, yet separately.

Miriam finished fixing the tea and brought both cups into the family room with her. Ray's eyes lit up when he saw she had two cups in her hand, knowing one of them was for him. He put the wedge of freshly cut wood onto the fire before taking the cup from her and sipping from it.

Miriam sat down on the oversized sofa and sank into the depths of the cushions, hoping it would warm her up soon. Ray put the poker down and closed the metal, mesh grating in front of the fire. He looked back at her, wondering if he should dare to sit with her, when he noticed her teeth chattering.

"You're still shivering," he said with concern, as he lifted a quilt from the end of the sofa and unfolded it over her.

He climbed in next to her and pulled her close to him. Within minutes, Miriam's shivering slowed as did her chattering teeth. She sipped her tea without mentioning the closeness between them, and he wondered how long she would allow it *this* time. He knew it was wrong for him to think such a thing, but he also wondered if she would continue to maintain her closeness with him even after she married Adam.

It suddenly dawned on Ray that Miriam—*his* Miriam would be Adam's wife, and the man would most likely expect her to be intimate with *him*. The very thought of it felt like someone had put his heart in a paper shredder. How could he just stand by and let Adam take Miriam from him? He couldn't stand the thought of another man holding her or kissing her and *more*. Would she cuddle up to him the way she was with him now?

A lump formed in his throat as he smoothed her hair. "I love you," he said quietly. "I'll always love you. I don't want you to marry Adam. I don't like the idea of him holding you the way I am now. I don't want you to kiss him the way you kissed me earlier. I don't want to let you go."

He watched her expression change in the soft glow of the firelight. Reflections of the flames flickered across her face, illuminating the tears that began to pour from her blue eyes. He could see that his words were finally beginning to have an effect on her, and he hoped it would help to change her mind.

"Don't ruin this," she said, sniffling back the tears. "Let's just enjoy the time we have together and try not to make more of it than it is. Hold me and make me feel safe and secure, even if it's only for this moment."

As tough as it was to concede, he would not fight her anymore. He would let be whatever would be, and accept whatever the outcome—no matter how much pain it caused him. For this moment, he would be content to hold her without any pressure for more.

Miriam set her tea on the lamp table beside the sofa and rested her head on Ray's shoulder. She looked up at him as his eyes closed. His breathing soon slowed and she felt the weight of him relax against her as he began to fall asleep. She closed her eyes, feeling the most comfortable she'd ever felt.

"I love you, too," she whispered.

CHAPTER 22

"Miriam Schrock!" a familiar voice woke her with a startling revelation.

She knew that voice.

"If *Daed* could see you now, you'd be in for a sound lashing for sure and for certain. In fact, I'm not opposed to dolling it out myself."

Miriam felt movement beside her—panicky, jerky movements, as if someone was in a hurry to move out of the way of something—or *someone.*

Was she dreaming?

Her eyelashes fluttered as she struggled to focus—on Ray, who was already on his feet and off the sofa where he was just lying beside her. How long had she and Ray been there? Her gaze followed the light streaming in through the large window behind the sofa.

It was *morning,* and they'd *slept* on the sofa *together.*

Her focus turned to the one calling her name for the second time. It was Benjamin, but how had he gotten into Claudia's home without their knowledge.

"It's a *gut* thing your *mamm* let me in here so I could witness for myself the sinful life you have made for yourself," he was telling Ray as he wagged his finger at him.

She wasn't dreaming!

Ray began to apologize to Ben, making excuses about them falling asleep and not meaning to.

Her *bruder* wasn't buying into any of it.

He waved a hand at Ray. "Save your lies for the Bishop. He will decide what really happened here."

He turned to Miriam, who was still half-asleep and trying very hard to process what was going on, while catching her breath and willing her heart to stop beating so fast. She stood up, gearing herself up to back-talk Ben, when morning sickness overtook her. She clamped a hand over her mouth and ran to the bathroom, Ben on her heels asking her what was wrong. She barely made it to the bathroom before the mere contents of her stomach spilled into the sink. She coughed and sputtered while her brother stood behind her, waiting for an explanation.

"What's wrong with you?" he asked. "Are you *pregnant?*"

"Jah," Miriam admitted as she grabbed a tissue and wiped her mouth. She turned on the water to rinse down the bile without looking up at him, a lump forming in her throat.

"From this *Englischer?*"

"Jah," she said. "But I'm marrying Adam Troyer, an Amish *mann,* so I can stay in the community."

"That's *narrish!"* Ben replied.

"That's what *I* told her," Ray chimed in.

Miriam looked at the two of them in the reflection of the bathroom mirror. "Both of you stay out of this. It's *my* decision what I do."

Ray looked at Miriam with narrowed eyes.

"Why won't you tell your brother that I proposed to you—several times?"

Ray turned to Ben. "I want to do right by your sister, but she's insisting on marrying the Amish man."

"If she's marrying the Amish *mann,* why did I find the two of you *sleeping* together?"

Miriam pursed her lips. "Don't talk about me like I'm not here."

Ben looked at Miriam with disgust. "You wrote in your letter that you were getting married. You didn't tell me any of *this.* Put on a clean dress and pull your hair up in your *kapp.* You look improper."

"There was nothing improper about what you saw. We fell asleep on the couch—that's all," Ray said in his defense.

"Then how did you manage to get her pregnant if the two of you haven't acted improperly?"

Miriam began to cry, and Ray crossed the threshold of the bathroom to stand behind her. He boldly pulled her toward him and rested a hand on her head to calm her. "She hasn't done anything wrong. I pressured her into *sleeping* with me, so if you want to blame someone, blame me!"

That wasn't entirely true and Miriam knew it, but she kept her mouth shut. She let Ray defend her honor, impressed by the protection he was giving her. As for her brother, he wasn't exactly supporting her, and that was his job as her older brother.

"Why can't you just be supportive?" she accused Ben.

"I won't be supportive of your sinful ways. You need to go to the Bishop and confess."

"I'm going to Sunday service with Adam the day after tomorrow, and I plan on giving a full confession at that time. Until then, do not judge me, dear brother!"

Ben hung his head. "What would *mamm* say if she was here?"

The mere mention of her adoptive mother brought fresh tears to her eyes. Oh, how she missed her.

"She would hold me in her arms and tell me she still loved me and that she couldn't wait to hold *mei boppli* in her arms too. I expect this behavior from your *daed,* but not from you, Benjamin Schrock."

"He's your *daed,* too."

Miriam shook her head, tears running down her face. "No, he's not. And you're not my brother. I only came to be with your family because my mother was in the same situation I'm in now. I imagine she was just as scared as I am right now—at a time when I should be able to count on family, I have none.

Claudia, Ray's mother, has been very kind to me and is very accepting of my *situation.* Even Ray has been more supportive than you are being. I'm marrying Adam so I can stay in the community, and keep my Amish heritage for my baby. Isn't that enough for you?"

At the mention of Adam and her impending marriage with him, Ray walked away, closing himself up in his bedroom.

Ben turned to her and issued her a warning.

"You're making a big mistake, and you should worry more about fixing it than about who is behind you. It looks to me like you have Ray, but you are hurting him with your *narrish* behavior."

"What are you talking about? I can't marry Ray, and I *won't.*"

"Fix this," he warned again. "When you come to your senses and realize that what you're doing is destroying a lot of futures, you let me know. In the meantime, I'll be at the B&B. I got a room there for a few days, unless you give me no reason to stay."

Benjamin turned his backside to her and stormed out of Claudia's house, leaving Miriam to cry it out on her own.

CHAPTER 23

"What are you doing here, Adam?" Miriam asked impatiently.

"I came to take you to the B&B so you can stay with your *bruder,* Benjamin."

"I told you yesterday that I'm not leaving here until the wedding, so you're wasting your time."

Adam took a step closer and whispered to her. "I don't want *mei fraa* sleeping with another *mann.* "

"I'm not your wife *yet,* and if you don't stop bossing me around, I won't be at all. I did not sleep with Ray. We were on the sofa, and he cuddled me because I was freezing, and we fell asleep in front of the warm fire. We were talking—that's all."

"You are not acting like a proper Amish woman. You won't last very long in this community. You already have several strikes against you for the lies you told about Nate, and now this. You will have a lot to confess on Sunday."

"Perhaps you should be worrying about your own confession, and never mind about mine. You've managed to upset me again, and I don't want to talk to you. Go home!"

She was *trying* to push his buttons. She was beginning to wonder if she didn't want out of this marriage, but she couldn't be the one to end it. He would have to do that for her. She just wasn't brave enough.

Adam threw his hands up in disgust and ran down the steps of the porch and hopped into his buggy. One click to the horse and he was on his way. At the moment, she didn't care if he ever came back.

৯৽৽৶

Miriam pulled her heavy coat around her, wishing she'd worn a scarf and mittens. She stuffed her cold hands into the small pockets of her coat, bending them against the stiffness to cover them from the wind. Light flurries bounced and swirled around her, catching in her eyelashes. She blinked them away, finding it increasingly hard to see in front of her as the snow thickened.

She didn't remember Ray's house being this far down the road, but she trudged along, the wind at her back, the hem of her long dress slapping against her wet calves. She had no way of gauging how far she'd already traveled, but surely she was close. If she didn't reach her destination soon, she would be soaked to the skin from the slushy snow that clung to her. It formed ice around the top rim of her boots and the cuffs of her sleeves, and was beginning to weigh down the pleats of her dress.

The sound of Ray's truck behind her caused her to turn around and stop. She waited for him to pull the truck over on the shoulder of the road. He leaned across the seat and pushed the passenger side door open and she hopped in without saying a word.

He turned the heater in the truck up so it blasted heat through the vents on the dashboard. "What are you doing out here without me? It isn't safe. You could have been hit or gotten lost. Visibility is not good in this thick snow."

"I was coming to see you," she said through chattering teeth.

He turned down the lane toward the house he'd purchased on Willow Creek. "I had to go into town for supplies and I stopped by the house to check on you, but you weren't there. My mother said you walked down the driveway, but you hadn't come back, so I came looking for you. What was so important that it couldn't wait until I came home tonight?"

"It doesn't matter," she mumbled, feeling suddenly foolish.

He pulled up to the house and parked the truck, and then turned in his seat to look at her. "You came out here in this weather for nothing?"

"Well, mostly, I needed some peace and solitude so I could do a little thinking. I figured I could get that on the walk over here. After all, I'm pretty confused right now, and I hoped I could talk to you about it. And for the record, it was barely snowing when I left the house. I had no idea it was going to turn into a blizzard."

Ray flipped his wipers before turning off the engine. "It is really coming down. Let's get inside and build a fire. We can talk then."

Grabbing the plastic shopping bags in the center of the bench seat of the truck by their handles, Ray hopped out of the cab and walked over to the passenger side. He assisted Miriam into the house and took the bags into the kitchen.

"I bought some groceries. Would you mind putting them away for me while I start a fire so we can warm up?"

She went into the kitchen—*her* would-be kitchen, and put away the items into the pantry and the freshly-painted cupboards. She looked around at the pale yellow walls and the white cupboards thinking it was just as she would have done it. The scalloped edge of the cupboard that wedged itself above the kitchen window boasted a yellow-checked curtain with perfect pleats. She opened the doors, noting the plates and cups were in the exact cupboards *she* would have put them in.

How did he know?

Was it possible these subtle likenesses were a sign that they were meant for each other after all?

CHAPTER 24

Miriam gazed upon the modern stove in Ray's kitchen, admiring the ease of its use as she made the two of them some hot cocoa. She could hear Ray in the living room tossing wood on the fire and stirring up the embers he'd obviously left from an earlier fire. Before long, the sound of popping and hissing filled her ears as the wood began to burn.

Carrying the hot cocoa into the living room, she couldn't help but admire the simple, antique furnishings he'd placed in the room. Tucked away in the far corner of the room, an Amish-made rocker sat so far back she hadn't noticed it until now. It caused a lump to form in her throat because it was an exact duplicate of the rocker her own *mamm* had rocked her in as an infant. Miriam set the cocoa down on the coffee table and went over to get a better look at the beautifully handcrafted piece.

She turned to Ray. "Do you mind if I sit here, or is this just for decoration?"

He gestured toward the chair. "No, not at all. Please sit in it. I bought it for you—well, for you and the baby."

Miriam couldn't say anything. She eased herself into the chair and leaned back, closing her eyes. She'd sat in her *mamm's* chair many afternoons with her eyes closed, imagining she was rocking with her. It was a game she often played in her mind that brought her comfort. Whenever she would find herself upset about something, or missing her *mamm,* Miriam would sit in that chair and rock until she felt better.

Now was one of those times, and this rocking chair was the closest thing she had to finding the answer to her problems—an answer that perhaps was right under her nose.

"Thank you for the hot cocoa," Ray said, interrupting her reverie. "What did you want to talk to me about?"

She looked at him blankly, uncertain of how to broach the subject. He'd been so kind to her that she didn't want to hurt him more than she already had.

"I know you don't want me to marry Adam. You've made that clear, but since *mei bruder* is here, it's more important than ever that I keep that *familye* bond and remain in the community. I will become Adam's *fraa* in only a few days, and I'd like to know how you want to handle the situation with the *boppli.*"

Her sudden change to the thick accent hadn't gone unnoticed.

She waited for him to protest, but he didn't say a word. He simply went about putting another piece of wood on the fire and poked at the coals as he stared at them. She could see his jaw clench, but he kept his focus on the task, not lifting his gaze from where he stared into the flickering flames.

"I'd like to still see you," he said without pulling his gaze from the fire.

"What do you mean?"

"Just because you're married to *him* doesn't mean you can't still spend time with me."

Miriam put her foot down on the hardwood floor to stop the rocker. "I've never been married before, but I doubt it's acceptable to *date* the *vadder* of your *boppli* when you're another *mann's fraa.*"

Ray whipped his head around and narrowed his gaze on her. "I don't see how it can be acceptable to marry another man when you are carrying *my* baby."

He had her there. She had no answer for that one. If she did, she probably wouldn't be in this predicament in the first place.

"You're right! It's not acceptable. It's not even logical. But I know it's what I *have* to do."

He crossed the room to where she sat, and knelt in front of her. *"Please* marry *me,* then."

Miriam cupped his handsome face in her hands. She hoped their child would inherit the sparkle in Ray's blue eyes, but more than that, his kind heart. She dipped her head toward him and pressed her lips to his.

He lingered there, sweeping his lips across hers.

He loved her, and it broke his heart each time she'd rejected him.

"You only want to marry me because of the baby," she said in-between kisses.

Ray stopped kissing her and stared at her with a stunned look on his face.

"What would make you think such a thing?"

Tears welled up in her eyes. "I brought up the subject of marriage to you after I found out I was pregnant, and you told me it would be a long time before you would be ready to get married."

"Is that why you tried to marry Nate?"

Miriam shook her head. "Amish marry early. The entire community helps the married couple, and help take responsibility for setting them up with a house and food and housewares."

Ray closed his eyes and let his forehead rest on hers. "I only meant I wasn't ready financially. But because things happened the way they did, I now have this house, and my new construction business, thanks to the help my father and mother gave me. My aunts and uncles gave us most of the furniture in this house. The *English* help each other too. In a way, the situation did me a favor. It made me grow up and take responsibility for myself. And now I want to be responsible for you and our baby—because I love you—not because I *have* to."

Miriam closed her eyes and breathed in the smell of firewood on Ray's skin. She loved him too, but did she dare tell him?

CHAPTER 25

Miriam hadn't even had a chance to talk to Ray before her brother was in her face, causing her anxiety about her poor judgment. Ray had excused himself to the barn so she could talk with Ben, but Miriam would have rather talked to Ray.

"Why is it that I come to see you at Claudia's *haus,* and I find you *here,* at Ray's *haus* instead?"

"I stayed here last night because of the weather."

"His *Englisch* truck won't drive in the snow?"

Miriam avoided his narrowed gaze on her and sat in the rocking chair. She leaned back and began to rock without saying a word.

Ben leaned down on his haunches in front of her and placed his hands over the arms of the rocker to stop it. His gazed followed the lines of the chair, inspecting it from the straight back to the rockers on the bottom.

"This is just like *mamm's* chair. Where did it come from?"

"Ray got it for me without knowing it was just like *mamm's.*" Tears welled up in her eyes. "He told me last night I could have it to take with me where ever I lived."

Ben stood up and crossed the room and leaned against the hearth for a moment, seemingly deep in thought. He picked up the poker and stirred coals before placing a new wedge of wood over them.

"It seems to me that Ray really loves you."

"*Jah,* but I need more than love. I need security. The kind you get from *familye* and the Amish community."

"It seems to me you have a *familye* right here, and all the security you need. Look at this *haus* Ray has gotten for *you.* He even went to great lengths to find an Amish-made rocking chair for you just like *mamm's,* without even knowing about hers. I imagine this *mann* would do just about anything for you, and you wouldn't even have to ask him."

Miriam resumed rocking. "Don't you think I already know all that? But I am torn. I want to do the right thing, but I am afraid to lose my Amish heritage."

"You can't have one foot in the *Englisch* world and one foot in the Amish community. You need to pick one or the other. You were born an *Englischer.* You are Amish only in your heart— along with *mamm.*"

"But I was brought up Amish," she argued.

Ben shook his head. *"Nee,* you were always an *Englischer. Mamm* knew it, and *Daed* sees it more now. I think that's why your relationship with him has suffered so much since *mamm's* death. You represent something she wanted so badly she challenged the rules of the Ordnung for."

"Are you saying *Daed* didn't want me?"

"Nee. I'm saying Amish don't adopt except within the community."

Miriam stifled a sob, choking down the lump in her throat. "I was facing having to give up my *boppli* for adoption, until I got the proposal from Adam. If I marry him, I won't have to do that."

Ben pulled her into his arms. "Don't cry little *schweschder.* Don't you see? You won't have to give up the *boppli* if you marry Ray either."

Miriam hadn't even considered that. Here she was, thinking marriage to Adam was the only way to keep her *mamm* from slipping away from her completely, and it was the only way to keep her *boppli.* Was it possible that she could have everything she wanted by marrying Ray? It couldn't be that easy, could it?

No.

If she married Ray, she would lose the community—and her only brother, who stood before her now trying to convince her to make a move that would remove him from her life.

"But I'd have to give up you and *Daed* if I marry an *Englischer.*"

He smoothed her hair, supporting her head against his shoulder. "You won't have to give me up. I'll support whatever decision you make. If *Daed* doesn't like it, I will have to visit you and Ray without him knowing. But I'm a grown *mann* capable of making my own decisions. *Daed* may come around in time, but until then, you will still have me."

His words brought some comfort, but additional worries. "What about the community?"

Ben walked her over to the sofa and sat down next to her. "When I talked to Claudia this morning, she told me about Ray's *familye* showering you with gifts for the *boppli.* You have a small community in Ray's *familye.* Why would you turn that away?"

Miriam stood up and paced the room.

"Because I want what's familiar. I *need* familiarity of *familye.* I'm not ungrateful for the beautiful store-bought quilts they gave me for the *boppli,* but it just isn't the same as the one *mamm* sewed for me."

Ben jumped up from the sofa and ran out the door, hollering, "I'll be right back," over his shoulder.

Before she realized, Ben was back inside the house, arms full of the quilt her *mamm* had sewn. She pulled it from him, burying her face in its worn folds and began to sob uncontrollably.

Ben steered her shaking frame toward the sofa and helped her sit down.

"If I'd known it was going to make you this upset, I wouldn't have brought it. I took it off your bed and brought it with me thinking it would bring you comfort while you recover from the accident."

Miriam lifted her face from the quilt. "I'm not entirely sad—I just miss her so much. I'm just crying because I'm so happy you brought me this. I didn't think I would ever see it again. It's the only thing I have of *mamm's,* and I was worried I wouldn't have it if *Daed* knew the *boppli's vadder* was an *Englischer."*

"Now you have it—no matter what your decision is."

Miriam hugged the quilt to her.

If only her decision could be this easy.

CHAPTER 26

Miriam heard the doorbell ring. It was something she wasn't certain she could ever get used to hearing. She hadn't heard a car or a buggy pull up into the long driveway, so she was curious as to who could be there waiting on the porch. She considered not even answering, but she couldn't do that in case it was someone important looking for Ray.

He'd gone into town to finalize some details with his construction crew, and Miriam missed him already. How was she ever going to get through the rest of her life without him? She wondered if she should consider *dating* Ray after she married Adam, just as he'd suggested. Could she do such a thing, even though their marriage was one of convenience alone?

When Miriam opened the door, it wasn't the cold and snow that took her breath away; it was seeing Bethany and Levinia in front of her that did it.

"Are you alright?" Levinia asked her. "You look very pale."

Miriam put her hand to her forehead and blew out a heavy sigh. "I think I might have stood up too fast. I feel like I'm going to faint."

"As long as it isn't from seeing us," Bethany joked.

Miriam thought she wasn't far off the mark as she sat down in the rocker.

"I see you got the rocking chair. When Ray spoke to your *bruder,* he described the one you had back home, and relayed the information to Ray so he could get it. He was very particular about what he wanted to get for you. I thought it was so romantic."

Miriam was suddenly confused.

"But *mei bruder* has only been here for two days, and when he saw it, he didn't say he'd helped pick it out. I wonder why he didn't tell me."

"Ray and Adam picked it up from Caleb Yoder yesterday afternoon. The Yoder's make all the furniture in our community. They have three generations who work on the furniture."

Miriam's eyes widened at the comment. "Adam went with Ray?"

Bethany nodded.

Were the two of them conspiring against her in order to force her to choose between them, or had they become friends? Either way, the idea of them spending time together for *her* benefit made her feel a little uncomfortable. But perhaps it was for the best. After all, they would both be raising her baby. She would rather have them get along than not, but she wasn't certain she relished the idea of them being friends either.

"You *do* know I'm marrying Adam and not Ray, don't you?"

"*Nee,*" Bethany said. "We assumed you were marrying Ray since he's the *vadder* of your *boppli.*"

Miriam practically choked on Bethany's words.

"I suppose Adam was waiting until Sunday service to have our wedding published," Miriam corrected them.

Levinia handed her a package wrapped in brown paper. "We made this for your wedding, but I'm not certain it will work now."

"*Danki,*" she said with downcast eyes.

Miriam took it, confusion filling her. She lifted the edge of the wrapping feeling a little awkward at opening a gift from two women who had plenty of reason to hate her—but yet they didn't. Forgiveness and peace were the Amish way, but she never thought much about it until now.

From the folds of the plain, brown wrapping, Miriam pulled a white, sheer pinafore with a swirl design embroidered into the silky material. It was the most beautiful pinafore she'd ever seen.

"We made it long-sleeved for the change in weather," Bethany said.

"It's *wunderbaar,*" Miriam said. "But much too fancy for an Amish wedding. Unless your Ordnung is more liberal than mine."

"*Nee,* it isn't," Levinia said. "But we were under the assumption you were marrying the *Englischer.*"

Miriam admired the simple elegance of the pinafore, her thoughts turning to Ray. She imagined the smile he would give her if he were to see her in such a beautiful garment. But in order for him to see her in it, she would have to marry *him.* Did she want to marry Ray? She liked the idea of it, but she was too afraid to even think about it.

"Try it on," Bethany urged.

"I'm so—grateful you made this—for me," Miriam stuttered, trying not to offend them. "But if I can't wear it to marry Adam in, there is no point in trying it on."

"Try it on," Bethany repeated. "We will need to make another one that is plain, but first, we will have to see if it needs to be altered."

"I suppose that makes sense," Miriam agreed, secretly eager to try on the elegant pinafore.

Miriam stood from the rocker, excused herself, and walked toward the bathroom. She turned back midway, remembering her manners, and addressed her guests.

"Would either of you like some hot *kaffi,* or cocoa?" she offered.

"*Nee,* we can't stay long," Bethany said.

Levinia stood and closed the space between her and Miriam, startling her by pulling her into a sincere embrace. "We only wanted you to have this gift from us, and to let you know that you *do* have friends here—no matter who you marry. After all, we have plenty of *Englisch* friends."

Miriam was filled with shock to her very core.

"You want to be *my* friend?"

"*Jah,*" they said in unison.

Tears welled up in Miriam's eyes. "I don't deserve your kindness. I've been so mean to you both."

"All is forgiven," Levinia said gently, giving Miriam one last squeeze.

"You are the most beautiful woman I've ever known," Miriam said through choked-back tears.

Levinia looked at Miriam curiously. To be called beautiful by a woman as beautiful as Miriam was the highest form of compliment she could ever get. But she quickly squelched her prideful thoughts, her crimson cheeks threatening to give her feelings away.

Within minutes, Miriam stood before the mirror in the bathroom at Ray's house—her house—if she wanted it. She admired how the pinafore hugged her narrow waist. Ray would certainly adore her in such a beautiful garment. She knew better than to give in to feelings of vanity, but at the moment, all she could think about was Ray, and the look that would surely cross his face when he saw her in this.

Her desire for him to see her was almost more than she could suppress. At the moment, all she wanted was to indulge in the feeling of adoration Ray would certainly have for her, and it felt comfortable. It felt right.

CHAPTER 27

Miriam wrung her hands, waiting for Adam to pick her up for the Sunday service. She'd donned her best pink dress, her *kapp* was set just right on her head. Her apron was neatly pressed, her hair twisted the same way she'd seen Bethany and Levinia wear theirs. The last thing she wanted to do today was to offend anyone in the community, and her appearance was critical.

Today would be a day of confession and remorse, and hopefully, forgiveness would follow. Her goal was to redeem herself in the community, and she was finally ready for whatever the day would bring. No matter what the outcome, she had to make things right with the community and clear her conscience.

As she exited her bedroom at Claudia's house, she passed Ray in the hall. His arms were full of boxes she supposed he'd packed from his room there. She knew he'd been slowly moving things into his new home, but she hadn't expected to see him this morning—especially not this early.

He leaned in and kissed her on the cheek.

"You look very pretty this morning. All that for me?"

Miriam's heartbeat doubled its rhythm, causing her to put an anxious hand to her chest for comfort.

"Adam will be here to take me to Sunday service in a few minutes."

No sooner had the words slipped off her tongue than regret filled her. Ray walked past her, but not before flashing her a hurtful look. When would she ever learn to control the filter between her brain and her mouth? For someone who'd decided she was going to stop hurting him, she was not off to a very good start.

Ray exited the front door. Miriam watched him toss the boxes into the snow-covered bed of his white truck that was very much in need of a good washing. A dirty layer of road-salt trailed the length from bumper to bumper, and mud clung to the tires. He leaned against the tailgate of the truck, his brow furrowed so deep, she could see it from the window from where she watched him. He was obviously not happy to hear she was still attending the service with Adam, but at the moment, this would be her only window to accomplish what she needed to do.

Though she was tired from lack of sleep, she was eager more than ever to get this over with. She'd stayed up with Claudia until well into the wee hours of the morning talking. In the end, she'd admitted to Claudia that she still loved Ray, and always would.

Miriam's decision was an easy one, and now it was time to put into action what was in her heart.

Adam's buggy pulled into the driveway. He hopped out and approached Ray. The two shook hands and exchanged brief pleasantries, while Miriam squirmed at the sight of it. The only consolation for her was that this unpleasant situation was all about to end.

Miriam threw her thick, wool coat over her shoulders and walked bravely out toward the two men, neither of them sure of their fate with her. She tried not to make any direct eye-contact with Adam, but it seemed Ray had the same intention for her.

She stopped short of Adam's buggy and turned to Ray, who hadn't left the tailgate of his truck. "Can we talk when I get back? I had intended to talk to you this morning, but I stayed up so late with your mother talking last night that I overslept."

Ray shrugged at the implied chip on his shoulder. "I don't see that we have anything to talk about. I asked you not to go to this service, and you've made up your mind to go no matter how I feel."

She took a step toward him, but noticed the apprehension in his expression. "I *have* to go to give my confession."

"I don't understand why."

"I don't expect you to understand, but I hope you will support my decision," she said.

Ray didn't want to hear what she had to say. She'd made up her mind, and he would have a hard enough time trying to live with her merciless decision, without her rubbing it in his face. There are certain things you just can't take back once they are said.

Flaunting Adam in front of him was nothing short of cruel, and he wanted no part of it. He was hurt, especially since he had been so sure he'd been able to get through to Miriam. He thought she loved him, but it was apparent she did not. He was confident she would choose him, but it was evident he was wrong about that too.

Miriam closed the space between them when Ray didn't answer. "I'm sorry, but this is something

I have to do. But I'd like to talk to you after I get back."

His jaw clenched. "I won't be here."

"Would it be alright if I came over to your house when I return?"

Ray looked off into the distance. "I'll be working on the barn all day. I don't think I'll have time to stop what I'm doing except to make a trip into town to the lumber store if I need to. Other than that, I'll be up to my ears with trying to patch the roof before nightfall."

Miriam knew now was not the time to get Ray to understand why she had to go to the service, or why she had to do what she felt she had to do in order to be able to live with herself. And she certainly was not about to have a detailed discussion about it in front of Adam. But she didn't want to leave things like this. She needed peace in her heart to prepare for what she felt was going to be the toughest decision she would ever have to make. In as much as Ray's support of her decision was critical to her well-being, Miriam suddenly realized she was not going to get it.

CHAPTER 28

Miriam listened to the rhythmic clip-clop of the horse's hooves as they passed yet another farm, while waiting and hoping Adam would open up a conversation with her. Even if it was only small-talk, it would be better than nothing. She couldn't waste the entire ride to the Yoder farm waiting for an opportunity to tell him what she needed to say. She had to say it *before* they arrived for the service. If not, she would lose her nerve.

She shivered a little, adjusting the heavy quilt to keep the bits of snow from gathering over her lap.

Adam saw her shivering and tucked his arm around her.

She gently pushed him away.

"If you're worried about being seen like this in front of others in the community, they will accept it once they hear the Bishop publish our wedding today."

Miriam bit her bottom lip, fear welling up in her.

It's now or never. I won't get a better opportunity than this. Lord, give me strength.

"The Bishop won't be publishing our wedding, Adam. I can't marry you."

She felt him become rigid in the seat next to her, his hands tightening on the reins.

"I was expecting you to say this. I'm not surprised, but I'm disappointed."

Miriam turned so she could look him directly in the eye. "Why would you be disappointed? You only offered to marry me as penance for the accident.

I forgive you for the accident, and I let you off the hook for having to marry me."

Adam glanced at her and then put his focus back onto the country road that was luckily devoid of traffic.

"What if I don't want to be let off the hook? What if I still want to marry you?"

A lump formed in her throat. "You don't *need* to marry me, and I don't believe you would *want* to marry me either. Don't you want to marry for love instead of obligation?"

Adam tried to put his arm around her again and she scooted away from him and shrugged his arm away.

"I could learn to love you."

Miriam sighed. "You shouldn't have to force yourself to love me. Love is something that comes naturally when you meet the one you are to marry. It is so far beyond your control that you can't keep it in no matter what, and you don't want to because all you want to do is be in that person's presence."

"I like being around you," he said defensively.

"You don't love me, and I don't love you. If we are to marry, that is what I would want for you *and* for me."

He turned to her, the horse following an instinctive path down the road without a lead. "We will take the time to court, then."

Miriam shook her head. "I don't have the luxury of time to court you. I'll be showing soon."

"Surely in a month you won't be showing enough to cause concern in the community. That would be enough time to see if we are compatible."

Miriam felt frustration rising in her. She wasn't getting through to him by being gentle with her words. She would have to shock him with reality.

"I don't want a marriage with someone I'm merely compatible with. I want to be married to someone I love. I love Ray that much, but I didn't realize it until I was faced with losing him."

Adam's expression changed.

She could see relief in his eyes.

"I am happy for you that you love Ray. I was still willing to marry you if it was necessary, but I understand now it won't be. If not for your honesty with me, I would have gone through with the marriage."

Miriam tilted her head against his shoulder.

"You are a *gut* friend, Adam. I will always be grateful to you for being willing to help me and the *boppli,* but it's time I grew up and accept what my fate is. I belong with Ray."

Adam gave her a quick, friendly squeeze. "I agree. But I suppose I need to take you back now—back to Ray. There is no reason for you to go before the community to give a confession since you will be living among the *Englisch* then."

"*Nee,*" she said. "Now it is more important than ever that I give that confession."

Adam looked at her curiously. "I don't understand why you would put yourself through that when you don't have to. A confession, especially a public one, can be nothing short of torture."

Miriam swallowed a lump of fear, pushing her worries aside.

"*Jah,* but I have made friends that I want to keep, and I can't do that if I don't make things right. I need to clear my conscience of the terrible things I did. I took advantage of your guilt over the accident and was willing to let you marry me out of guilt—all for my own selfish reasons—most of which I've made up in my head. I came close to ruining Nate's life with Levinia, and now I could have ruined your life if I'd have let you go through with this fake marriage.

I have hurt too many people with my lies, and I want to be the sort of honorable person my friends can respect. The kind of person that learns from mistakes and makes every effort never to repeat them. I want Ray and *mei kinner* to be able to respect me, too. More than that, I want to be able to respect *myself,* and I won't ever be able to do that if I don't change my heart and do what's right."

"I'm proud to call you *friend,* Miriam," he said in a most sincere tone.

Tears welled up in her eyes at his words of comfort. It was just what she needed to give her the strength to face the community.

CHAPTER 29

Miriam twisted at the long tendrils she'd freed from her prayer *kapp*, waiting for Ray to answer his door. She didn't know why she felt the need to ring the bell, but after the way she'd left him two hours ago, she feared she'd ruined her chances with him.

Lord, please put forgiveness in Ray's heart for me the same way you did for the Amish community. Danki for blessing me with the words I needed to convey my remorse for my sins against them. Bless me with the same words now to make amends with the mann I love.

Ray opened the door, looking surprised to see her. "I didn't really expect to see you back here."

Trying not to cry, Miriam fought to find her voice. "I told you I needed to talk to you, but I had to address the Amish community first—to make amends."

Ray took a step back. "Well come in out of the cold and snow."

Miriam waved off Ben, who'd driven her, and watched as he steered Adam's buggy around the circle drive and down the dirt lane to the main road. After, she followed Ray into the house. She paused before sitting on the sofa, wishing she could sit in *her* rocking chair just once more—in case Ray rejected her and sent her on her way.

"Would you like some coffee or cocoa to warm you up a bit?" he asked as he stoked the fire.

"No—thank you." Miriam stood up nervously and walked over to the hearth and held her cold hands out toward the warm flames. It was something to occupy herself while she gathered her thoughts.

"I came to apologize for the way I've treated you, but I beg you to listen to why I did what I did. I'm not trying to make excuses for my behavior, because I take full responsibility, but I need you to know the reasons behind it." She looked up at him to be sure he hadn't lost interest.

"First, and most importantly, I want to say how deeply sorry I am for not trusting you with the news of the baby. I got scared when I found out I was pregnant, and after the accident, I was even more terrified when they confirmed the pregnancy because it meant I had to make some hard decisions."

Ray guided her back to the sofa and wrapped a quilt around her shoulders. "I wish you would have included me in those decisions. Maybe then we wouldn't be in this mess."

"I was afraid if I didn't stay in the Amish community, I would have to give the baby up for adoption the way my mother did to me. The Amish community was the only place I felt safe. But now I realize, Ray, that you would do anything you could to make me feel safe and to be sure we didn't have to give up our child."

"I would think my constant proposals and this house would be enough to make see that I would do anything for you and our child."

Miriam wanted to ask if he would still have her, but she didn't dare at this moment.

"I know, and I'm sorry for that. If only I'd trusted you more, things could have been different."

Discouragement furrowed his brow. "I told you the moment I found out that I would raise our baby with you. Why didn't you believe me?"

She could see the hurt in his eyes.

"It wasn't that I didn't believe you, after a long talk with your mother last night, she helped me to realize I have what she calls "trust issues". And even though I had never heard of such a thing, her explanation did make the most sense of anything I was feeling."

Ray chuckled. "I can see that. My mother can talk circles around anyone, but she only does it because she cares."

"I adore your mother, and I pray that I will still get a chance to be her daughter-in-law." Miriam knew it was a risky thing to say, but she couldn't take it anymore. She *had* to know if there was still a chance for her and Ray to be together and raise their child.

Ray pulled her into his arms. "I think I can arrange that."

Miriam was almost too afraid to hope she wasn't dreaming this moment with him.

Suddenly, Ray jumped up from the sofa and slid down on one knee in front of Miriam. "I suppose I should officially *ask* you."

Tears of joy threatened to choke her, but she swallowed them down, trying hard to contain her emotions.

Ray took her hand in his and pressed a kiss on the back. "Miriam, will you bless the remainder of my days by becoming my wife—my *fraa?*"

"*Jah,*" she said as tears spilled from her eyes.

Ray leaned up and pressed his lips to hers. It was the kind of kiss that could only be felt with the love that filled her heart for him. He was loyal to the very core of his being; how could she not love him? He was everything she needed and more—much more. She hungered for this man's love, but she would be hungry no more. He was hers; mind, body, and soul. Her heart would always belong to him, but at this moment, all she wanted to do was to claim his soft lips.

She swept her mouth across his, her hands to each side of his strong jaw. His whiskers prickled her fingertips, the feel of his manly flesh arousing delight in her. She would love him for the rest of her days and never let him go.

CHAPTER 30

Miriam fidgeted while Claudia's hairdresser piped baby's breath in-between her curls to form a flower "crown" around her head. The woman had made up Miriam's face conservatively, and surprisingly, the makeup covered the scar on her face completely. She stared at her reflection, noting how beautiful she looked, but she couldn't help but think how much she'd changed on the inside—where it counted the most. She was happy with the person she was now—a feeling she'd never experienced before. Claudia had complimented her on the progress she'd made, and she had to admit she was finally proud of herself for her accomplishment in that area.

When the hairdresser was finished fussing over her, Miriam let her out of the room at the B&B, and then slipped the silky pinafore over her head that Bethany and Levinia had made for her. Though it wasn't traditional Amish, it wasn't traditional *Englisch* either. It was sort of a mixture of both, but she liked the fact that it was Amish-made. Made by two new friends who had come to see her marry the man she loved.

Claudia entered the room and presented her with a beautiful bouquet of yellow roses, sheer, white ribbons hanging from it that matched her pinafore.

"No *English* bride can be without a bouquet to hold at her wedding. It helps to hide your shaky hands!"

Claudia hugged her soon-to-be daughter-in-law just before she left the room.

She hadn't thought of the traditional bouquet, but she would be happy to carry it. Happy because Claudia had been thoughtful by presenting it to her.

Her brother poked his head into the room just then. "They tell me you need someone to *give you away.*"

"*Jah,*" she said, feeling a little choked up at the offer. "I would like that very much *mei bruder.*"

"I know it's tradition for a *vadder* to do this job, but I will gladly step in for him since he couldn't be here. I'm not certain if he will ever come around, but I will always be your *bruder,* no matter who you marry."

Miriam didn't want to cry today.

She wouldn't.

She would be happy that her adoptive brother was with her, happy with the new family she was about to gain, with the friends she had earned through her change of heart, and with the man she loved more than anything, who was about be hers for the rest of her life.

After a quick hug, Ben took Miriam's hand and led her out into the large meeting room of the B&B, where her wedding would take place in only a few moments.

As she took her place at the doorway, the traditional *Wedding March* was played on the piano. With her arm tucked in the crook of her brother's elbow, Miriam stepped along the blue rug between the rows of chairs toward her new husband.

Miriam's eyes locked onto Ray, her handsome husband-to-be. The dark grey suit he wore hugged his six-foot frame, his blond hair pushed up in front just the way she liked it.

Ray was her goal, her future.

His smile washed away every last fear she had left in her. There was no doubt in her mind she was doing the right thing. She was confident she would have a good life with Ray, and that he and his family would take care of her and their baby just as well as even the largest Amish community would. She knew she wasn't losing the community; she had friends now that would support her. She couldn't help but think that she and her baby would have the best of *both* worlds.

Though Miriam would live and raise her baby in the *Englisch* world, she would forever remain Amish in her heart.

THE END

Look for Book Three: Sweet Nothings

Available now

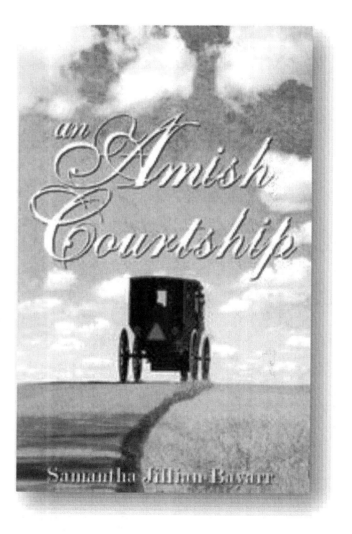

Available now

Other Titles by Samantha Bayarr

Jacob's Daughter Amish Series
Jacob's Daughter
Amish Winter Wonderland
Under the Mulberry Tree
Amish Winter of Promises
Chasing Fireflies
Amish Summer of Courage
Under the Harvest Moon

Amish Brides of Willow Creek Series
Amish Brides of Willow Creek: Sibling Rivalry: Book One
Amish Brides of Willow Creek: Second Chances: Book Two
Amish Brides of Willow Creek: Sweet Nothings: Book Three
Amish Brides of Willow Creek: Snowflake Bride: Christmas Edition

Amish Winter Collection
An Amish Christmas Wish
Amish White Christmas
Amish Love Letters

LWF Amish Series
Little Wild Flower: Book One
Little Wild Flower: Book Two
The Taming of a Wild Flower: Book Three
Unto Others: Companion Edition
Little Wild Flower in Bloom
Little Wild Flower's Journey

The Quilter's Son series
The Quilter's Son: Book One: Liam's Choice
The Quilter's Son: Book Two: Lydia's Heart
The Quilter's Son: Book Three: Nathan's Apprentice
The Quilter's Son: Book Four: Maddie's Quilt
The Quilter's Son: Nellie's Legacy
The Quilter's Son: Ethan's Pride

Christian Romance
Milk Maid in Heaven
The Anniversary
A Sheriff's Legacy: Book One (Historical)
Preacher Outlaw: Book Two (Historical)

Made in the USA
Lexington, KY
04 February 2017